C000171965

Writing Essentials

A Teacher's Guide to Grammar, Punctuation and Word Usage

Dianne Bates

amba
press

© 2024 Dianne Bates

Published in 2024 by Amba Press.

Previously published in 2017 by Hawker Brownlow Education.

Terms of use for this publication

This work is copyright. Apart from fair dealings for the purposes of private study, research, criticism or review, or as permitted under the Copyright Act 1968 (Cth), no part should be reproduced, transmitted, stored, communicated or recorded, in any form or by any means, without the prior written permission of the copyright owner. Any enquiries regarding copyright or permissions must be made to Amba Press.

Some pages in this book are marked as reproducible. You may be entitled to reproduce these pages for educational purposes under Part VB of the Copyright Act, or for government purposes under Part VII Division 2 of the Copyright Act 1968, on the following conditions:

1. You are the purchaser, or the employee of the purchaser, of this publication, AND

2. Each copy is used solely for your teaching purposes

Amba Press
Melbourne, Australia
www.ambapress.com.au

ISBN: 9781923116573 (pbk)
ISBN: 9781923116580 (ebk)

Printed in Australia

A catalogue record for this book is available from the National Library of Australia.

Contents

Introduction

As all teachers know, writers need correct grammar, punctuation, word usage, and a knowledge of vocabulary to express themselves. That's why it is important for those who are working with young students to teach these skills. Teachers should demonstrate how punctuation and grammar are tools writers use to communicate their ideas clearly to readers. And too, they should show how correct grammar and punctuation help to convey meaning accurately, enhance readability, convey professionalism and attention to detail, enhance credibility and authority, and facilitate communication. As a teacher, you need to convey to students that if they are having trouble getting an idea to come out the way they want it to, they might want to look at how they are constructing and punctuating their sentences.

Another aspect teachers should focus on is vocabulary as it is a crucial component of language proficiency and plays a vital role in self-expression, understanding others and overall communication. It helps readers to understand complex concepts and to communicate effectively. Thus, as a teacher you are wise to let your students know that having a strong vocabulary can dramatically improve their reading and writing ability.

One of the easiest, most effective, and most enjoyable ways for students to improve their use of grammar, punctuation and vocabulary is to read. Remind your students that every time they read, they should pay attention to grammar and punctuation conventions. They should ask themselves where are these authors placing commas? Where are they using punctuation to separate sentences, phrases or ideas? How are they formatting lists, quotations or long sentences? Teach students to use the structures they see in their reading as models when they write. The more they read, the more they will be able to recognise and adopt effective uses of grammar and punctuation. Reading, of course, is also one of the main ways of enriching a student's vocabulary. Ideally, when a student come across a word that they're unfamiliar with in a book, they should look up its meaning in a dictionary, thereby adding a new word to their vocabulary.

Writing Essentials: A Teacher's Guide to Grammar, Punctuation and Word Usage features:
- Information about the fundamentals of grammar and punctuation
- Types of vocabulary
- Exercises (in grammar, punctuation, word usage and vocabulary) for students to test themselves.
- Answers to the above exercises

Grammar

Nouns

A noun is a word used for naming a person, an animal, a place or a thing. There are four different kinds of nouns:

- A **common noun** names a person, place or thing. Words like 'woman', 'country', 'day', 'month' and 'book' are all common nouns.
- **Proper nouns** refer to a particular person, place or thing. They always begin with a capital letter. 'Nancy', 'Australia', 'Monday', 'March' and 'The Bible' are proper nouns.
- **Abstract nouns** describe things that cannot actually be seen, heard, smelt, felt or tasted. Examples of abstract nouns include 'love', 'war', 'freedom', 'energy' and 'justice'.
- A **collective noun** describes a group of people, animals or things, for example: a *flock* of birds, a *herd* of cows, a *deck* of cards, or a *bunch* of flowers.

Exercise G 1:

Identify the nouns in the following sentences. What kind of nouns are they?

1. The reason I didn't go to church on Sunday is that I was dining at Mrs Graham's place.

2. Give Stanley my love when you see him in Sydney.

3. After a good night's sleep, my neighbours Stan and Shirley caught a limousine that took them to the airport.

4. I had so much more energy after eating a meal of fine food, including meat, vegetables and cheeses.

5. Carol and I are going on holiday to Greece in September.

Exercise G 2

Identify the nouns these sentences. Which of them require capital letters?

1. The doctor came on the last friday in april.

2. The author f. scott fitzgerald wrote a novel titled *the great gatsby*.

3. Every year many people go to london in england to see buckingham palace, queen elizabeth's home.

4. My friend ashley met sir hubert stanley when she was in fiji.

5. My parents mr and mrs reynolds live in australia but I live in canada.

Singular and Plural

A **singular noun** names just one person, place or thing, for example, 'child', 'window' or 'box'.

A **plural noun** indicates that there is more than one, as in the words 'children', 'boxes' or 'windows'.

The plurals of nouns may be formed as follows:

1. By adding 's' to the singular:

Singular	Plural	Singular	Plural
shoe	shoes	niece	nieces
key	keys	spoonful	spoonfuls
lay-by	lay-bys	dog	dogs

2. By adding 'es' to nouns ending in 'x', 's', 'ss', 'ch' or 'sh'

Singular	Plural	Singular	Plural
box	boxes	gas	gases
church	churches	princess	princesses
octopus	octopuses	inch	inches

3. By adding 'es' to nouns ending in 'o'

Singular	Plural	Singular	Plural
tomato	tomatoes	hero	heroes
potato	potatoes	veto	vetoes
motto	mottoes		

Note – *There are exceptions to the rule above, including:*

Singular	Plural	Singular	Plural
piano	pianos	solo	solos
taboo	taboos	zero	zeros
radio	radios	shampoo	shampoos
dynamo	dynamos	tattoo	tattoos

4. By changing the 'y' after a consonant into 'ies'. (Remember: 'a', 'e', 'i', 'o' and 'u' are vowels. All the other letters are consonants.)

Singular	Plural	Singular	Plural
lady	ladies	army	armies
city	cities	berry	berries
story	stories	spy	spies
theory	theories	curry	curries

Note: If the 'y' follows a vowel, we follow the ordinary rule and add 's'.

Singular	Plural	Singular	Plural
boy	boys	guy	guys
play	plays	toy	toys
key	keys	day	days

5. By changing nouns ending in 'f' or 'fe' into 'ves'

Singular	Plural	Singular	Plural
half	halves	loaf	loaves
calf	calves	knife	knives
wharf	wharves	shelf	shelves
wife	wives	life	lives

Note – There are exceptions to the above rule:

Singular	Plural	Singular	Plural
roof	roofs	chief	chiefs
hoof	hooves	staff	staffs
gulf	gulfs	proof	proofs
belief	beliefs	dwarf	dwarfs

6. By changing the inside vowels:

Singular	Plural	Singular	Plural
man	men	goose	geese
woman	women	foot	feet
tooth	teeth	mouse	mice
stratum	strata	nucleus	nuclei
fungus	fungi/funguses	crisis	crises

7. Some words take 'en' or 'ren'

Singular	Plural	Singular	Plural
child	children	ox	oxen

8. Some nouns have the same singular and plural form:

advice	deer	information	news	series
baggage	fish	knowledge	salmon	sheep
cattle	furniture	music	scenery	species

9. Some nouns are used in the plural only:

athletics	ethics	news	riches	
clothes	goods	people	pants	series
contents	gymnastics	politics	shorts	
economics	mathematics	pyjamas	thanks	

10. In compound nouns, you add 's' as follows:

Singular	Plural	Singular	Plural
brother-in-law	brothers-in-law	Lord Justice	Lords Justice
looker-on	lookers-on	passer-by	passers-by
sister-in-law	sisters-in-law	son-in-law	sons-in-law

11. Some English words have unusual plural endings that reflect their original roots in foreign languages such as Latin, Greek and French:

Singular	Plural	Singular	Plural
abacus	abacus	medium	media
addendum	addenda	Mister (Mr)	Messieurs (Messrs)
appendix	appendices	Madam	Mesdames
apex	apexes	nucleus	nuclei
bacterium	bacteria	oasis	oases
basis	bases	plateau	plateaux
beau	beaux	radius	radii
cactus	cacti	stimulus	stimuli
criterion	criteria	stratum	strata
datum	data	syllabus	syllabuses (syllabi)
focus	focuses (or foci)	tableau	tableaux
formula	formulae	trauma	traumata
index	indices	vertebra	vertebrae
larva	larvae	vortex	vortices

Exercise G 3

What are the plurals of the following nouns?

1. bluff
2. leaf
3. salmon
4. commander-in-chief
5. archipelago
6. duty
7. minus
8. mosquito
9. dynamo
10. antithesis
11. criterion
12. energy
13. synopsis
14. minimum
15. ash
16. prince
17. erratum
18. furniture
19. thief
20. cliff
21. diagnosis

Pronouns

Pronouns take the place of nouns in a sentence. Instead of referring to a person or thing by its actual name, you can use a pronoun instead.

There a number of different types of pronouns:

- **Personal pronouns** refer to oneself and others. The words 'I', 'you', 'me', 'she', 'he', 'we', 'they' and 'it' are all personal pronouns.

- **Possessive pronouns** indicate ownership, as in the words 'yours', 'mine', 'his', 'her' 'its', 'ours' and 'theirs'

- **Reflexive pronouns** are used to indicate that someone is performing an action on themselves. Examples of reflexive pronouns include 'myself', 'yourself', 'himself', 'itself' and 'themselves'.

- **Relative pronouns** include 'who', 'whom', 'whose', 'which', 'that' and 'what'. They are used to establish a relationship between two nouns, or to tell us more about a specific noun for example, The house *that* Jack built, or The woman *who* went fishing.

- **Interrogative pronouns** include 'who', 'whose', 'whom', 'which', 'that' and 'what'. These pronouns are used when asking questions.

- **Demonstrative pronouns** point to a specific thing or group. Pronouns such as 'this' and 'these' indicate something close by, whereas 'these' and 'those' point to something further away. For example, I don't want *this* here, I want *that* there.

- **Indefinite pronouns** are words such as 'any', 'each', 'several' and 'some'. These refer to people generally, rather than specifically.

Personal pronouns can indicate a particular point of view: The first person (I, me, we), the second person (you), and the third person (he, she, it, they). When using several personal pronouns in a sentence, start with the third person, then the second person and finally the first person, e.g. Barry, you and I are going to the zoo.

 Exercise G 4

Find the pronouns in these sentences and work out what type of pronoun they are:

1. We left the room to search for them.

2. She asked him if he knew any of the people.

3. It isn't your book, it's mine!

4. Whose book is it?

5. Are these the animals that belong to him?

I and me

In some sentences it is difficult to decide whether to use 'me' or 'I'. Should you say 'me' or 'I' in this sentence: "Katherine and (I / me) go to school"? Whenever you find it difficult to decide, try splitting the sentence into two short sentences, like this:

> **Katherine is going on holiday. I/me am going to school.**
>
> **The correct sentence is "Katherine and I are going to school".**

After prepositions (words that show place such as 'on', 'before', 'between' or 'under'), you always use the object form of the pronoun. In this sentence: It is a secret between Bill and (I/me), the correct word to use is 'me', and so the correct sentence is: It is a secret between Bill and me.

 ## Exercise G 5

Use the correct pronouns in the following sentences:

1. My dog and (I/me) are going for a walk.

2. When can Julie come with him and (I/me)?

3. She and (I/me) have decided not to go.

4. That is a secret between Lyn and (I/me).

5. He put the books in front of (I/me).

Prepositions

Prepositions are words which show the relationship of one thing to another. They can also tell us when something occurred. Some examples of prepositions include 'under', 'in', 'down', 'past', 'into', 'over', 'across', 'beside' and 'up'. Prepositions are always attached to a noun or pronoun, for example, The food is *on* the table, or, Ron goes walking *after* dinner.

 ## Exercise G 6

Find the prepositions in the following sentences:

1. The children climbed into bed before saying their prayers.

2. Gerry walked across the road to buy groceries from the store.

3. Jett jumped over the fence, ran past the house and up some stairs.

4. Under a tree lay a cat licking its fur.

5. After breakfast, Fred put on his boots and went for a run in the park

Adjectives

An adjective is a word that tells you more about a noun or pronoun.

There are five types of adjectives:

- **Descriptive adjectives** are the most common. They describe nouns. Words such as 'red', 'cold', 'soft' and 'beautiful' all belong in this category.

- **Interrogative adjectives** are used to ask questions. 'Which' or 'what' are good examples.

- **Possessive adjectives** indicate ownership, for example 'his', 'her', or 'their'.

- **Adjectives of number or quantity** describe how much, or how many. Examples include 'six', 'any' 'a dozen' and 'half'.

- **Demonstrative adjectives** indicate the specific noun you are referring to. 'This', 'that', 'these' and 'those' are all demonstrative adjectives.

An adjective usually comes before a noun, but sometimes it can be separated from its noun and come afterwards, for example, Daisy looked *worried,* or, My school principal can be very *fierce.*

 Exercise G 7

Find the adjectives in the following sentences and identify their type:

1. My silly sister behaved badly and annoyed many people.

2. That sour-faced woman wants dozens of green vegetables.

3. Does your friend have any of those exercise books?

4. Which of the black pens and drawing pages do you want?

5. When Toby hurt his big toe, he screamed for mum to help him.

Making Comparisons

Many adjectives can be used to compare two or more nouns. For example, the word 'large' :

large is an **ordinary** adjective; 'larger' is a **comparative** adjective; 'largest' is a **superlative** adjective.

Note: Where adding 'er' and 'est' would make an adjective awkward, you form the comparative and superlative by putting 'more' and 'the most' in front of it, e.g. She is beautiful; she is *more* beautiful; she is the *most* beautiful.

Exercise G 8

Work out the comparative and superlative forms for the following adjectives:

1. tall
2. smart
3. good
4. thin
5. little

6. many
7. much
8. pretty
9. ugly
10. grey

Verbs

Verbs include doing, thinking and saying words as well as states of being and having:

- **Doing verbs**: I *swim*, or, I *rode* a pony to the fair.
- **Thinking verbs**: She *knows* his name, or, He *was worried* about the man.
- **Saying verbs**: She *spoke* angrily to her students, or, All the children have *been told* how to behave.
- **Being or having verbs**: The police officer *is* in the station, or, Ashley *has been* to school

Exercise G 9

Identify the verbs in the following sentences:

1. The small children played happily in the cubby-house.
2. The students were given their assignments.
3. The boys will go mountain-climbing next week.
4. Ricky has had a bad chest infection.
5. When she was ill, Emily thought she might die.
6. The horse galloped around the arena and then jumped the fence.
7. Iris can do the cooking tonight.
8. Did you make the bed this morning?
9. Children enjoy playing on computers.
10. Tigers roam jungles and are hunted by poachers.

Tenses

All actions occur at a particular time: this is referred to as "tense". The tense of a verb tells you the time at which the action takes place.

There are three main tenses:

- The **present tense** shows action happening now, for example, I *eat*/I *am eating*, or, he *eats*/he *is eating*.

- The **past tense** shows action happening before now, as can be seen in, I *ate*/I *was eating*, or, they *ate*/they *were eating*.

- The **future tense** is action which will happen, for example, tomorrow I *will eat*/I *will be eating*, or, He *will eat*/he *will be eating*.

 ## Exercise G 10

Use the correct tense of the words shown in brackets in the following sentences:

1. Next week I (stay) in the hospital.

2. Right now I (demand) your attention!

3. Last night I (sleep) at my aunt's place.

4. Our teacher (make) us work hard.

5. Tom (polish) his shoes this morning.

6. Tomorrow night we (eat) at the new restaurant.

7. She (swim) up and down the pool's lanes.

8. Ted does not (approve) of killing animals.

9. The giggling of the girls (annoy) the boys when they were in church.

10. As I (drive) along the road, a horse (appear) in front of me.

Auxiliary verbs

Auxiliary verbs help the main verb to express various aspects of tense, voice, mood and other precise meanings.

There are 25 auxiliary verbs:

may	be	is	do	have	should	will	am	ought
might	being	was	does	had	could	can	are	dare
must	been	were	did	has	would	shall		

- I *have been* told about that.
- She *had dared* to behave badly.
- Jenny *ought to have* come.
- He *was used to* getting his own way.
- *May* I borrow your pencils?

 ## Exercise G 11

Identify the auxiliary verbs in the following sentences:

1. He isn't going.

2. I was asked to attend the concert.

3. Julia is doing her homework.

4. Alex should be handling this problem.

5. We need to see the doctor as soon as possible.

6. Oscar will have done his cleaning by noon.

7. Jessica has done the sweeping.

8. I can help you carry the luggage.

9. The officer was capturing the burglar.

10. The principal will help parents learn about their children.

Participles

Participles are parts of verbs. They help to form the tenses of verbs and usually follow the auxiliary verbs 'to be' and 'to have'.

There are two kinds of participles:

- A **present participle** is part of the verb which ends in 'ing'. For example, My uncle is com*ing*; Tomorrow we are *going*; or, Dad has been *mowing* the lawn all morning.

- A **past participle** usually follows 'was', 'has', 'have' and 'had'. For example, I *was allowed* to go; Brian *has walked* home; Mike *had slept* all night.

  Past participles usually end in 'ed' (e.g. talked), 'd' (e.g. heard), 't' (e.g. burnt), 'en' (e.g. chosen), or 'n' (begun).

Participles can be adjectives as well as adverbs. For example, We watched the *rising* moon, or, She was a *calming* influence on her foster son.

Exercise G 12

Identify the participles in the following sentences:

1. I have conquered my greatest fear: the fear of flying.

2. Daylight has begun and soon it will be time to leave.

3. As he patted the dog, Paul was soothing it.

4. Claire had slept restlessly all night.

5. We watched the children who were sitting around the fire.

6. The wounded and the dying were carried from the battle-field.

7. Having finished his meal, Chris went out.

8. I saw a star shooting across the sky last night.

9. We are going to Canberra by bus tomorrow.

10. Have you been watching the boiling eggs?

Gerunds

When the present participle is used as a noun, it is called a gerund. Gerunds are formed by adding 'ing'. For example, The *screaming* of the children annoyed the adults, or, The *capturing* of the bushranger shocked the villagers.

As a gerund acts like any other noun, it can be described by an adjective, as can be see in The *ceaseless* wailing of the baby distressed its mother, or, The *energetic* bouncing of the boy exhausted him.

 Exercise G 13

Identify the gerunds in the following sentences:

1. I don't like the sound of loud shouting next door.

2. What do you think about the sounds of drumming he's making?

3. The noisy roaring of the car engine upset the neighbours.

4. She heard the sound of vacuuming coming from her bedroom.

5. Alice received falling marks in English.

Adverbs

An adverb usually tells you more about a verb. It modifies any word in a sentence, other than a noun or pronoun. An adverb nearly always answers the questions:

- *How much?* (really; almost; too; very; rather)
- *When?* (never; always; regularly; now; soon; after)
- *Where?* (outside; away; beside; under)
- *Why?* (to learn her lesson; to see the Queen; to give a report)

An adverb can be one word or a group of words. Most adverbs end in 'ly' and come from adjectives, for example, easy, easily; happy, happily; smart, smartly.

Adverbs are highlighted in the following sentence:

Julie drove **home** (where) **quickly** (how) **yesterday** (when), **to collect her bags** (why).

Adverbs of degree indicate intensity, for example, It was *too* cold to go outdoors; My brother looked *very* different in his new coat; or Bill came home *extremely* tired last night.

Sentence adverbs can change the meaning of a sentence. They include words and phrases such as 'moreover', 'however', 'nevertheless', 'on the other hand', and 'despite'.

 ## Exercise G 14

Identify adverbs in the following sentences:

1. Life is difficult; moreover, you need to work hard in order to succeed.

2. When the train arrived early, hundreds of people pushed forward to get out of it quickly.

3. We were only able to get half of the groceries despite having plenty of money.

4. She felt, however, that the teacher was not as smart as she was.

5. He chatted to the girl in a friendly way and smiled pleasantly to strangers.

Voice

There are two different ways you can arrange verbs in a sentence. These are often called "voices".

The **active voice** shows that the subject of the verb is performing an action, for example, *Jim asked* me to come to school, or, *A stranger kidnapped* them.

The active voice is stronger and more direct than the passive voice. The active is used much more often in writing because it is easier to read, shorter and easier to understand.

The **passive voice** shows that the subject is having an action done to it, e.g. *I was asked by* Jim to come to school; *His supper was eaten by* Julie, or, *They were kidnapped by* a stranger.

Public notices are often written in the passive voice because it appears less demanding than the active. A notice in a park may use the passive, "Dogs must be kept on a lead", which can seem more polite and less demanding than the active construction, "Keep your dog on a lead!"

Exercise G 15

Identify whether the following sentences are in the active or passive voice. How would you rearrange each sentence to create a different voice?

1. Six meals were cooked by granny.

2. Jack laughed at Jill.

3. The plants are watered every day by the gardener.

4. A taxi was ordered to take the family home.

5. Dad mowed the lawn early this morning.

Sentences

A sentence is a group of words which makes complete sense on its own. There are different kinds of sentences:

- **Statements** are sentences which state facts, e.g. Our family has a red car.

- **Questions** are sentences which need an answer, e.g. Does your family own a car?

- **Commands** give orders or requests, e.g. Get out of there now!

- **Exclamations** express a strong emotion, e.g. Wow, you look gorgeous!

Sentences always start with a capital letter and end with a full stop, question mark or exclamation mark, depending on the type of sentences they are.

Exercises G 16

Decide whether the following sentences are statements, questions, commands or exclamations.

1. After midnight my family and I drove to the city.

2. Do you enjoy playing tennis?

3. Make a cake and do it now!

4. What an amazing sight!

5. How many people attended the concert?

6. There is a small bridge over the river.

7. How stupid of her to forget!

8. Hang on!

9. It's dangerous to climb that tower.

10. With a choking cry jack fell to the ground.

Subject and Object

The **subject** of a sentence is the person, animal or place that the sentence is about, for example, *The house* stands in a paddock, or, *Ray* is my brother. The subject can also show who is performing an action in a sentence, e.g. *My brother* swims every day.

The **object** tells you what or whom the verb in the sentence affects, for example, Dogs chase *cats*, or, He put *his boots* under the table.

Pronouns that are used as subjects of verbs are: 'I', 'she', 'he', 'we', 'they' and 'you', e.g. *He* is running away, or, I don't know if *they* will come.

Pronouns that are used as objects of verbs (or prepositions) are: 'me', 'him', 'her', 'us', 'them' and 'you', e.g. Give the book to *them*, or, During the footy match, I tackled *him*.

Exercise G 17

Find the subject in each of the following sentences:

1. Davis is the boy who scored the winning try.

2. Gene and I are going to the football match.

3. When are you and Mum heading for the beach?

4. I put the cat and dog into the car.

5. Every Christmas Santa Claus visits our house.

Identify the object in each of the following sentences:

6. A frightening thing happened to him and me.

7. She ate the baked dinner.

8. Grandpa put his socks in the drawer.

9. Dogs chase cats.

10. Caspar was driving the car when it crashed.

Clauses

A clause is a group of words which contains a verb. It is part of a sentence. Look at this sentence:
"Claudia went to school because she was eager to learn." It contains a **main clause** (Claudia went to school) and a **subordinate clause** (because she was eager to learn).

A **main clause** can stand by itself and make sense.

A **subordinate clause** is dependent on the main clause for its meaning.

Like phrases, clauses can do the work of adjectives, nouns and adverbs in a sentence. Clauses add details and interest to a sentence.

Look at these kinds of clauses:

Adjectival clauses often begin with 'who', 'whom', 'which' or 'that', e.g. The boy *who had the longest hair* was seated in the barber's chair, or, That dog *with the curly tail* belongs to my friend Peter.

Adverbial clauses do the work of an adverb by answering the questions **How?** (He sang *as loudly as he could*); **Where?** (Percy examined the book *in the library where he works*); **When?** (They called out *as they passed our house*) and **Why?** (She took three boxes *as she needed to fill them.*)

 Exercise G 18

Identify clauses in the sentences below:

1. The water was icy and the current was raging.
2. Jean tried to run to safety but the storm prevented her.
3. Unless he gets help, it will be too late.
4. The car, which carried two passengers, drove into town.
5. I wanted to go to the concert but my mother wouldn't let me.
6. This is the book that I own.
7. I hoped to attend the market which was held in the gardens.
8. I wanted to play the piano but she beat me to it.
9. Unfortunately I can't play because I've broken my finger.
10. I used to know the boy whom my classmates nicknamed Rusty.

Phrases

A phrase is a group of words that makes sense but is not a sentence. It does not contain a verb. Examples of phrases include: 'with a laugh', 'into the ocean', 'up the hill' and 'beside the river'.

There are three kinds of phrases:

Adjectival phrases are used in place of adjectives, e.g. The boy *with a smile on his face* spoke to the woman *in the car*.

Adverbial phrases act as adverbs. They answer the questions How? Where? and When? about the verb. For example, He answered *in an angry voice* and chased the culprit *behind a building*.

Noun phrases contain a noun and all the words that "go" with it. It can consist of just one word, as in the phrase, *Greed* is not good, or, in a group of words, such as *Bags of money* lay on the table.

 ## Exercise G 19

Find the phrases in these sentences:

1. The mother of four children leads a very busy life.

2. With a big splash Jim fell into the lake.

3. All of a sudden, Jade fell off the slippery dip.

4. After the questions, the mayor replied with much enthusiasm.

5. When we go out, we usually head for the city.

6. All the people in the room began to stamp their feet on the floor.

7. The dog with black and white spots fetched the stick for its master.

8. When the baby cried for its mother, the nurse went to its aid instead.

9. On his birthday, Ricky had a cake with chocolate icing and strawberry cream.

10. The helicopter hovered above the building before landing on the roof.

Conjunctions

Conjunctions are words used to connect other words together. The other words might be phrases, clauses and sentences. Some conjunctions include:

although	because	however	though	whether
and	before	if	whenever	
as	but	nevertheless	where	

Exercise G 20

Choose an appropriate conjunction to connect the following sentences:

1. She went to the shops. There she bought two new shirts.
2. Ann likes coffee. Vicki likes tea.
3. Mark got up late. It was Saturday.
4. The girl was laughing. She was crying.
5. Tony has a car. He will go to town.
6. She felt ill. She did not stop working.
7. He was angry. His father was late.
8. Emma went to bed. She cleaned her teeth.
9. He acted stupidly. He acted like a monkey.
10. Will you stay here? I need to go somewhere.

Interjections

Interjections, also known as exclamations, are words used to express surprise or enthusiasm. They are always followed by an exclamation mark, e.g. Oh!, Hello!, Wow!, Fantastic!, Way to go!

Sentences: common problems

1. When writing a sentence, it is imperative that there is agreement between verb/s and subject in person.

    -   A singular pronoun such as 'she' takes a singular verb such as 'gives', as in, *She gives* me a lift every day.
    -   A plural subject takes a plural verb, for example, *They give* me eggs from their farm.

2. A singular subject (such as 'each') takes a singular verb: *Each* person *is* willing to fight for the cause, or, *Everyone* who fights *is* keen to do so peaceably.

3. There should always be agreement with a noun that is the subject of the verb. For example, A *book* of rules *appeals* to keen players, or, The *wind* from the highlands *is* blowing hard.

4. When subjects are joined by 'and', the plural verb is used, for example, John *and* Mary *are* husband and wife, or, The prisoner *and* his cell-mate *were* in trouble with the warders.

5. When subjects are joined by 'and' but we think of them as a single entity, the singular verb is used, e.g. *Fish and chips is* popular at the footy, or, *Rock and roll is* the best music of all!

6. When a collective noun is used, the verb is singular, e.g. A *herd* of cattle *is* charging down the hill, or, The *flock* of cockatoos *has* flown into the gum tree.
    - Note: When using collective nouns where the subject is thought of as individuals, the plural verb is used, e.g. The *police are* only human, after all, or, The *staff are* all enjoying the morning tea.
    - When the word 'number of' is used as a collective noun, we use the singular verb, e.g. The *number of* people here *is* astronomical.
7. The verb should always agree with its subject, e.g. She is *one of the girls* who *know* him, or, Debra is *one of the few writers* who *think* as I do.

Exercise G 21

Choose the correct verbs in the following sentences:
1. Swimming is one of the sports that (attract/attracts) me.
2. A number of scholars (have/has) won admission to University.
3. A herd of animals (is/are) stampeding across the plains.
4. Salt and pepper (are/is) on the table.
5. The birds of summer (is/are) flying into our garden.
6. Everyone who (want/wants) to come (is/are) welcome.
7. He (smoke/smokes) every day – a silly habit!
8. Each of the boys (is/are) responsible for the silliness.
9. The flock of birds (have/has) taken off.
10. (Are/is) red, yellow and blue the colours you use to create secondary colours?

Paragraphs

A paragraph is a set of sentences. There is no strict rule about how many sentences there should be in a paragraph, but each paragraph should help your reader by introducing new information into your story such as a new person, a change of time, a change of action, a change of place and so on. The idea is to end one paragraph and begin another at a point where it is logical to have a break.

The first line of a paragraph is indented (starting further from the margin than the rest of the text) to make it easier to see where each paragraph begins. The exception to this is when you are writing the first paragraph of your story, or you have left a space between paragraphs to indicate time passing and you are starting a new paragraph. In these cases, your paragraph is left-aligned.

When you are writing dialogue, you should take a new paragraph for each new speaker. See the section on quotation marks on page 24 for examples of this.

✎ Exercises G 22

Read the following and break it into paragraphs:

Hi! It's me, the Easter Bunny! Easter's just come and gone. Did you get your eggs a few days late? If you did, I'm truly sorry. It was not my fault. The fact is I was kidnapped and forced to spend the whole holiday period inside a bedroom cupboard. My kidnapper, Jonathon Livermore, (known as J.L.), tried to deliver the eggs. But he messed up the whole thing. You're probably asking what sort of a person would kidnap the Easter Bunny the thing is J.L's not really such a bad kid. He was trying to make friends. But he went about it the wrong way and mucked things up. I first met J.L. behind my chocolate factory dressed in a cowboy suit, he was playing by himself, trying to lasso a fence post. I was stacking crates of last-minute Easter egg orders when he saw me. "Hey!" he yelled, "come over here!" I took one look at him and turned away I had no time for loud-mouthed little boys. "Come and play with me!" he demanded I took no notice he strode up. "Play with me!" "I'm busy", I said. "Go find a human your own age to play with."

Puncuation

Capital letters

A capital letter should always be used for:

- *The beginning of a sentence*, for example, We went for a drive in the country.

- *The beginning of a paragraph*

- *People's names*, such as David, or Bert Young

- *Names of places* like Sydney, Australia, Murray River, Mount Kosciusko, (but not for points of the compass, e.g. north, south, east, west)

- *Names of streets, roads and special buildings*, for example, Kulgoa Road, West Avenue, The White House

- *Headlines or titles,* however, smaller words – such as 'the', 'of', 'but', 'or' and 'and' – are not given capitals, e.g. *The House of the Rising Sun*, or, *Home on the Range.*

- *Days of the week, months of the year and special days*, like Monday, March, Easter (but not the names of seasons)

- *Titles given to special people*, for example, President, Prime Minister, Lieutenant Snow, Princess Ann

- *The name of spiritual heads or religions*, including God, Our Father, Mohammed, Buddha, Hinduism

- *The word 'I' is always a capital letter*, as in, I think I will go to the fete, *not* i think i will go to the fete.

- *When writing the address on a letter*, e.g. Lady P Bernard
  Waratah House
West Street
Bondi

 Exercise P 1

Read the sentences below and identify the places where capital letters are needed:

1. *under the boardwalk* is a song by the rolling stones.

2. *robbery under arms* was written by a famous novelist.

3. have you read *confessions of a liar and thief?*

4. *i love a sunburnt country* is a poem by the australian poet dorothea mackellar.

5. the choir sang the national anthem, "advance australia fair".

6. while on holiday in new york, america, sandy and I went to the top of the empire state building.

7. my friend who i meet the first tuesday of every month is princess marcia james.

8. while visiting henry last october, I was lucky enough to meet his grandmother who lives on randwick road.

9. every summer my family goes on holidays to wollongong nsw.

10. the countess of york presented me with a trophy. later the countess and i had dinner together.

Full stops

Whether it is long or short, a sentence needs a full stop at the end. Full stops mark a definite pause and are used at the end of all sentences, except where a question mark or exclamation mark is used.

Sentences usually have a noun and a verb. For example, My dog chases cars; however, they can sometimes consist of only one word, especially when spoken phrases like "Hello".

After a full stop, a capital letter is always used to begin the next sentence, for example, We went bowling. After that we went out to dinner.

 ## Exercise P 2

In the passage below, identify five places where a full stop should go. It can be helpful to first read it aloud while taking note of where you naturally pause.

She had hiked for hours her head ached and she was thirsty when she reached the next road she decided to take the left fork she felt pleased with her decision when she arrived at the motel it had been a long trek

Abbreviations

An abbreviation is the shortened form of a word using some of the letters or just the initials, e.g. Jan, *January* or Dr, *Doctor*

Here are some other common abbreviations:

Mr *Mister*	St *Street*	Revd *Reverend*	PS *post script*	am *ante meridian*
pm *post meridian*	e.g. *example*	i.e. *that is*	Capt *Captain*	OMG *Oh my god!*

Commas

A comma is used to make sentences – particularly long sentences – easier to read. When you are reading a sentence aloud, commas usually mark a slight pause. There are numerous ways to use commas:

- When things are **written in a list**, commas are used. For example The school canteen sells chips, meat pies, sandwiches and juices. Note that a comma is *not* used after the last item in a list.
- Often when you **name someone** or something and **add a description**, a comma is used between the name and the description, as in the sentences, Jim, my guinea pig, escaped this morning, or, Bill owns a dog, Sassy.
- Commas are also useful **to join words** in a sentence: for example, where a phrase or clause has been added or where two sentences made into one, for example, with a loud bang, the gun went off, or, Although it wasn't deep, the river was dangerous to swim in.

 ## Exercise P 3

Where would the commas go in the following sentences?

1. Peter teases his sister annoys his parents and frightens the neighbours.

2. She stopped regained her breath looked behind her and then went on running.

3. The monster had crossed eyes a warted nose purple cheeks a crazy haircut and fifteen fingers on each hand.

4. The huge beast as big as an elephant lumbered through the jungle.

5. With a splash the stick hit the water and the dog dived in for it.

Semicolons

A semicolon marks a bigger break than a comma, but it is not as final as a full stop. It can go between two sentences (which a comma cannot) and should be used if the sentences are alike, or belong together, for example, This part of the river is cold; be prepared! or, Some boys like to fight; some like to fight more than others.

Only use semicolons when you want a strong break between two parts of a sentence.

Note that unlike a full stop, a semicolon always comes in the middle of a sentence.

 ## Exercise P 4

Put semicolons where needed in the following sentences:

1. Penny tried to ride the horse it wasn't easy as she was inexperienced.

2. The first step to cooking on a barbeque put on your apron.

3. At the concert we saw a band playing rock and roll an acrobat who was amazing a singer with a husky voice and a magician whose act went terribly wrong.

4. The girl was like her sister long-legged blonde and very shy.

5. He always took short cuts as a result he often became lost.

Colons

A colon is used before giving an example – or examples – of something, as in, There's something I ought to tell you: I can't swim, or, At school we did terrific activities: softball, art and running relays.

Colons are also used between two sentences, when the first makes a statement, and the second one says what you mean by it, e.g. Both times Pat was lucky: her Dad was there to help her.

Colons can be found before instructions: How to ride a bike: first hop onto the bike and put your feet on the pedals.

 ## Exercise P 5

Place colons in the correct places in these sentences:

1. You have only one person to blame yourself.

2. There are two rules you must keep your room clean and pick up your belongings.

3. There's one thing my brother's good at getting into trouble.

4. If you want to find out go to the shed and check out the shelves.

5. Here is what I think you only get one life so take good care of it.

Quotation Marks

We use quotation marks to indicate speech. They are like inverted commas and can be single or double, e.g. 'Ouch!' or "Ouch!"

Inside the quotation marks, you write exactly what is said, plus any punctuation that goes with it – full stop, comma, exclamation mark or question mark.

Using quotation marks with other punctuation can take some getting used to. First, open the quotation marks and then write the words that are spoken. Next, add punctuation to the end such as an exclamation mark, question mark, comma or full stop before you close the speech marks. The punctuation you use will depend on what and how something is said.

An "attribution" or, "dialogue tag" is a small phrase to show who is speaking and how they are saying it. They can appear before, after or even in between dialogue. 'Said', 'cried' and 'asked' are common attributions. When interrupting a line of spoken text with an attribution, first close the quotation mark, then add a comma (see the first quotation in Example 2).

When you have a new speaker, you need to take a new paragraph.

Example 1:

"Come this way!" Brian cried. "I think I can see a way out."

"Do you think we'll make it?" asked Jill.

"Of course we will. Just follow the track and we'll be there soon."

Example 2:

"I am pleased to announce", said the teacher, "that class is finished for the day."

"Do you mean we can go now?" asked Judy. "Not at three thirty?" She was amazed at the news.

The teacher looked at her. "Of course; you can go now."

 ## Exercise P 6

Use the correct symbols to punctuate the following sentences:

1. I have won said Linda a trip for two to America we'll be going next week
2. Trinity said I can't believe it's true are you kidding me
3. Would I tell a lie Linda replied of course it's true
4. You lucky thing her sister said I wish I could come
5. Well you can't said Trinity it's only for mum and me

Brackets

Like quotation marks, brackets come in pairs with words, phrases or sentences inside them. Brackets are used as follows:

- To show an **interruption**: I met John (he is a doctor) and told him I was a nurse.

- To make an **explanation**: The house was empty (everyone had gone overseas) and so we made ourselves at home.

- To add an **afterthought**: I will bake a cake (if that's all right with you).

When you use brackets, it is sometimes difficult to decide exactly where to put commas, full stops and other punctuation marks. What can help is to first work out how you'd punctuate the sentence without the brackets, and then insert the bracketed section.

If the words in a bracket make a complete sentence and come between complete sentences, put a full stop inside the second bracket, Remind me tomorrow. (It is so important for you to remember.) Then we can make a final decision.

 Exercise P 7

Identify the places where brackets and other punctuation are needed in the following sentences:

1. Chris, Bill and Pat Pat is a home-maker are all coming to dinner.

2. At the party were Elysse, Andrew the boy I told you about and Marg.

3. After the drive, we returned the car a Holden ute to the garage.

4. Barry spent fifteen minutes far too long trying on a pair of boots.

5. During the tour they visited numerous cities but why not, I wondered, Paris and London in just ten days.

Dashes

Dashes are sometimes used **to mark a big break, or interruption**, in a sentence: Ray turned five – more than three months ago, or, Sam dialed emergency – not for the first time in his life.

Sometimes a dash can be used **like a colon**: Which department do you want – men's wear or haberdashery?

Sometimes dashes are used **instead of brackets**: The old bridge – the one over the river – should have been repaired years ago.

Dashes are also useful for **showing where someone is interrupted**, and doesn't finish what they're saying: "I've been telling them for years that –" Suddenly we were interrupted.

 Exercise P 8

Work out where dashes are needed in the following sentences:

1. His sister skipped school so she said.

2. My mother's car the one she drives every day needs repairs.

3. They tell me he is an angry kind of man I don't know him.

4. Sandwiches, pies, tarts all of these were for lunch.

5. Who do you want to speak to Jerry or Terry?

Hyphens

A hyphen (half the length of a dash) is used to **link two or more words together** to make one word or expression, 'Blue-eyed', 'do-it-yourself' and 'happy-go-lucky'.

When two or more words are joined together, they are called **compound words**. There are **compound nouns**, e.g. water-wheel, or dog-house. And **compound adjectives**, e.g. four-footed, or green-eyed.

Hyphens are used **to write numbers and fractions** that are more than one word, e.g. ninety-two or four-fifths.

You can use hyphens to **make a group of words into an expression**, e.g. good-for-nothing, or man-about-town.

Exercise P 9

Identify where hyphens are needed in the following sentences:

1. Carl is green eyed, big nosed and bird brained.

2. When I did the problem, my answer was twenty five and three quarters.

3. Dad is a do it yourself handyman who is over eager to please Mum.

4. The man eating lion performed tricks in the circus in front of wide eyed children.

5. He was an ex army officer who is now retired as he is a semi invalid.

Ellipses

An ellipsis (plural, ellipses) is a series of three full stops, sometimes known as "omission marks". They are used to suggest that something is missing from a text, either within or at the end of a sentence, e.g. Where the ... does she think she is? or, I promised to tell the truth, the whole truth and nothing but ...

An ellipsis has many uses: to show halting dialogue, to trail off, or to close an endless list, e.g. The numbers read 20, 30, 40, 50, 60 ...

Exercise P 10

Work out where ellipses are needed in the following sentences:

1. Well, I was going, but then

2. What the is he doing with that knife?

3. Mark crashed to the floor only much later did he come to.

4. The problem was, would the lawyer go to court, or

5. I bought two cakes for ten dollars at that price I could have made five myself.

Apostrophes

An apostrophe looks like a comma but is raised off the line of writing, e.g. that's.

Apostrophes are used to **replace missing letters in contractions**, e.g. The contracted form of "do not write" is "don't write", while the contracted form of "could not write" is "couldn't write".

An apostrophe also goes after an owner's name to **show something belongs to them**.

If the owner is singular, put the apostrophe at the end of the word and add an 's', e.g. Carl's jumper.

If the owner is plural, or the word ends in 's' already, just put the apostrophe after the 's' that is already there, e.g. Thomas' dog.

If the plural does not end in 's', you still add an 's', then the apostrophe, e.g. elephants' trunks.

 Exercise P 11

Identify where apostrophes are needed in the following sentences:

1. After the run we put the dogs coat on it and then we went to Marks place.

2. Thats the girl I told you about who doesnt go to school.

3. We cant come to Angus party next week because were going on holidays.

4. Its impossible to tell whether or not its alive.

5. That is James dog and Susies cat.

6. The dog sat and scratched its back leg.

7. The man stole the ladies handbags.

8. She went to get the mens hats and the boys scarves.

9. Im going to have to get the two cats dinner.

10. Were afraid shes going to be too late for the shows opening.

Punctuation in poetry

Poets often use punctuation in unusual ways. Some (like the American poet e e cummings) don't use it at all. The usual way to write poetry is in lines and verses (also known as *stanzas*). Often (but not always), the first word on each line begins with a capital letter, even if it isn't the start of a sentence. And not all lines start flush against the left margin; poets often use different indents to give their verses a "shape".

Exercise P 12

Take the following poem by Christina Rossetti and punctuate it as you might if it was your own poem. Include indents to give your poem a "shape". Compare your attempt with Rossetti's actual layout. Which poem shape do you think works best?

who has seen the wind neither I nor you but when the leaves are trembling the wind is passing through who has seen the wind neither you nor I but when the trees bow down their heads the wind is passing by

Bullet points

A bullet point, usually shown as a heavy dot (see below) may be used to separate items in a list, e.g.

- Vocabulary
- Word usage
- Punctuation

Where a bullet point introduces a full sentence, it is usual to begin with a capital letter and end with a full stop or semicolon, for example:

- My father cooks well.
- My mother is a solicitor.
- My sister sings in a choir.
- My brother is in a soccer team.

Asterisks

An asterisk (shown as *) is used to draw the reader's attention to a footnote, or to show that certain letters have been omitted, usually to indicate swearing, as in, Some bas***d hit me!

Word Usage

Common Errors

Writers beware! Several words in the English language are often misused or spelled incorrectly. Below you'll find an alphabetical list of words that frequently trip up aspiring authors.

About and around

About means approximately or roughly, e.g. My grand-father is about ninety years old. There were about forty people at my party.

Around means on all sides or in a circle, e.g. The ball spun around and around. The soldiers gathered around the garrison.

Affect and effect

Affect is a verb, e.g. How did the hot weather affect you?

Effect is a noun, e.g. The hot weather had a poor effect on us.

A well-known way of remembering this rule is by using the acronym, **RAVEN** – **R**emember: **A**ffect **V**erb, **E**ffect **N**oun.

✎ Exercise W 1

Decide whether you should use 'affect' or 'effect' in each of these sentences:

1. To _____ a change, we must employ a new teacher.

2. The _____of the hail was to damage our home.

3. The strike _____ the way we travelled into town.

4. We felt the _____ of cuts to our water supply.

5. What was the _____of possums in your roof?

Among and between

Among is used when referring to more than two people, e.g. In this strange land we live among natives.

Between is used when referring to two people, e.g. We shared the sweets between the brother and sister.

Exercise W 2

1. Mum divided the cakes _____ Shelley, Mikki and Aaron.

2. I can't decide from _____ the hundreds of choices.

3. I have to choose _____ Jack and Rick for my team.

4. We walked _____ the many trees in the forest.

5. I live my life _____ my mum's house and my dad's house.

Articles: A, an and the

'A', 'an' and 'the' are known as "articles".

You use 'a' and 'an' with singular nouns, e.g. a book, or an umbrella.

'The' (known as a "definite article") can be used in front of all nouns, singular or plural, e.g. the book, or the umbrellas.

When something is first referred to, 'a' or 'an' is used. 'The' is used when referring back to something, e.g. I saw a dog that I'd like as a pet. The dog has brown fur and a black tail.

You use 'an' where the following word starts with a vowel sound ('a', 'e', 'i', 'o' or 'u'), e.g. an apple; an egg; an ink-spot; an orange; an uncle or an honest person.

 Exercise W 3

Choose where to insert 'a', 'an' or 'the' in the blank spaces below:

1. Bill went for _____ walk up a long track. _____ track led to _____ mountain.

2. Penny owns _____ dog, _____ owl and _____ cat you saw yesterday.

3. Pass me _____ pear, please. Yes, _____ green one will do.

4. Pam has _____ small doll. _____ doll went missing yesterday.

5. It is _____ honour to serve you.

Bought and brought

Bought is the past tense of the verb 'buy', e.g. I bought a dozen eggs at the supermarket.

Brought is the past tense of the verb 'bring', e.g. He brought a bunch of flowers to the house for his mother.

Exercise W 4

Choose whether the sentences below require 'bought' or 'brought'

1. We spent two dollars and_____ a loaf of bread.

2. What have you _____ to sell at the market?

3. Max and Ann have _____along their old clothes.

4. He _____ a fast, roomy, new car.

5. I was surprised when he _____ along a dinosaur bone for the display.

Bring and take

Bring should be used when something is being moved towards the speaker, e.g. I will bring the lunch for you.

Take should be used when something is being moved away from or with the speaker, e.g. When I go camping, I never know what to take.

Exercise W 5

Choose whether the sentences below require 'take' or 'bring':

1. I shall _____ my cat when I go on holidays.

2. _____ your cat to me.

3. I must _____ my medicine with me.

4. Shall I _____ her some cake?

5. When are you going to _____ your project to school?

Can and may

Can indicates ability to do something, e.g. I can drive a car.

May asks permission, e.g. May I have the last biscuit in the jar?

Exercise W 6

Decide whether 'can' or 'may' belong in the blank spaces below:

1. _____ you help me with these equations?

2. _____ I go to the toilet?

3. _____ Jill and I take the last cakes?

4. _____ you direct me to the highway?

5. _____ I spend fifty dollars at the shops, Mum?

Continual and continuous

Continual means repeated often, e.g. No-one likes continual interruptions when they are trying to sleep.

Continuous means without a stop, e.g. All night we were forced to listen to the continuous music.

Disinterested and uninterested

Disinterested means impartial or free of motives, e.g. In listening to a criminal case the judge needs to be disinterested.

Uninterested means showing no interest, e.g. Although it plays all the time, I am uninterested in modern music.

Double negatives

Two negatives equal a positive so they are usually avoided, e.g. "I didn't do nothing right" means I did do something right. Here's another example: "I didn't never do well in exams", which means I did do well in at least one exam.

 Exercise W 7

How would you rewrite these sentences to avoid using double negatives?

1. I didn't do nothing.

2. I don't never go to the movies.

3. Can you never not do anything right?

4. I wasn't not going.

5. Give me that or I will never give you nothing.

Either and or

The verb in connection with "either ... or" agrees with the nearest subject, e.g. Either the boss or the workers are to blame, or, Either the workers or the boss is to blame.

 ## Exercise W 8

Choose the correct verb in each of the following sentences:

1. I'm going to (choose/chose) either these tools or those.

2. Either you or Emily (is/are) coming with me.

3. Either the man or the women (is/are) catching the bus.

4. Which do you prefer: either the boys or the girl to (act/acts) as our mascot?

5. Either Mum or Dad (want/wants) to know the answer.

Good and well

Good is an adjective, e.g. She is a good girl; It seems good to me; You're looking good.

Well is usually an adverb, e.g. He did well in his exams; She is well-loved by her family; The children were well-dressed.

Note: The word 'well' can be an adverb, an adjective, a noun or a verb.

 ## Exercise W 9

Decide whether 'good' or 'well' is more appropriate in each sentence:

1. Did he do _____ when he was competing?

2. We found that it was a _____ piece of pie.

3. She did _____ to please her mother.

4. Heath writes _____.

5. She is _____-mannered.

Less and fewer

Less refers to a quantity that cannot be counted, e.g. My sister does less homework that me.

Fewer refers to a number that can be counted, e.g. There are fewer people living in Australia than in India.

 Exercise W 10

Use 'less' or 'fewer' to fill in the blank spaces

1. There is _____ sugar in this bag than that.

2. In our country there are _____ sheep than in your country.

3. Our teacher gave us _____ homework than yesterday.

4. Because of good signage, there are _____ deaths on the roads.

5. As I'm on a diet, I now eat _____ fat than I ate before.

Lend and loan

Lend is a verb, e.g. He plans to lend me some money

Loan is a noun, e.g. He gave me a loan of ten dollars.

 Exercise W 11

Choose either 'lend' or 'loan' to fill in these sentences:

1. Do you think he'll _____ me his book?

2. Ray gave me a _____ of his book.

3. When we get to school, I'll ask to have a _____ of the homework answers.

4. Give me a _____ of that case or I'll report you.

5. I'm going to _____ him my favourite computer game.

Lie and lay

To *lie* means to not tell the truth: I lie, I am lying, I was lying, I lied or I have lied.

It can also means to rest: I lie, I am lying, I was lying, I lay, or I have lain down.

To *lay* means to put something down (lay a table, lay an egg, lay the plate on the table). I lay, I am laying, I was laying, I laid or I have laid the plate on the table.

Exercise W 12

Choose the correct form of 'lie' to insert into the blank spaces:

1. When he finished _____ the books down, he picked up his pen.

2. Is he _____ or is he telling the truth?

3. Because I was tired, I _____ down.

4. All afternoon Granny has _____ on the lounge.

5. Pop has already _____ dishes on the dinner table.

Must have

At times people mistakenly say or write **must of,** probably because it sounds like the contraction **must've**. The correct term is **must have**.

Neither and nor

After using **neither**, use **nor** rather than **or**, e.g. Neither this tie nor that one is suitable.

The verb after "neither ... nor" follows the closest subject in number, e.g. Neither the boy nor the parents were there, or, Neither the parents nor the boy was there.

Note: The plural verb is used after singular subjects when the idea they express is plural, e.g. Neither bread nor butter are good for dieters.

Exercise W 13

Use the correct verb in each of the following sentences:

1. This tool suits neither the (needs/need) of the mechanic nor his offsider.

2. Neither Tom nor his sisters (is/are) in the house.

3. I (want/wants) neither the apples nor the banana.

4. Neither the boys nor their sister (is/are) playing indoors.

5. Instead of the cake, they (prefer/prefers) sandwiches.

Past and passed

Passed is a verb, e.g. We passed the ball from player to player; The truck passed the petrol station.

Past can be used as a noun, adjective, preposition or adverb, e.g. Grandparents are always talking about the past; The fortune teller talked about past lives; The horse galloped past the stable; Past the winning line flashed the runner.

 ## Exercise W 14

Use either 'passed' or 'past' to complete the following sentences:

1. We strolled _____ the derelict houses.

2. He _____ the ball from his friend to his teacher.

3. The runner was first _____the line.

4. He is well _____ the age of retirement.

5. Under the bridge he dawdled, over the hill and _____ the barn.

Shall and will

You use **shall** and **will** when you are writing in the future tense, e.g. I shall, we shall, you will, she will, they will. Notice that 'shall' is used with first person pronouns ('I' and 'We'), and 'will' is used with second and third person pronouns ('you', 'he', 'she', 'it', 'they'). Here are some examples:

I shall go to the shops tomorrow; They will travel overseas next month.

You also use 'shall' and 'will' when you are showing determination. In this case, the opposite rule is applied; 'shall' is used with second and third person pronouns and 'will' is used with first person pronouns, e.g. I will, we will, you shall, he shall, she shall, they shall.

While this is the traditional usage, the word 'shall' is becoming less common, and is often interchangeable with 'will'.

Here are some examples:

You shall leave, right now! I will not listen to a word you say.

Exercise W 15

Choose either 'will' or 'shall' to complete these sentences:

1. I _____ try even harder to get first place in class.
2. We _____ arrive at your place this afternoon.
3. She _____ catch the bus tomorrow morning.
4. I _____ bake a cake for the fete, just you wait and see!
5. The girl covered her ears and said, "I _____ not do it!"

Stationary and stationery

Stationary means not moving, e.g. The train is stationary.

Stationery refers to writing paper, pens and pencils, e.g. The student bought stationery at the store.

They're, there and their

They're is the shortened form of 'they are', e.g. They're coming with us.
There shows place, e.g. Put the book over there.

Their is used to show ownership, e.g. They put their coats in the closet.

Exercise W 16

Choose either 'they're', 'there' or 'their' to fill in the spaces below:

1. Do you know if _____ going to the show?
2. The children put _____ toys away after playing.
3. Sally and Todd arranged for _____ car to be cleaned.
4. Don't put it _____!
5. Sit with that woman over_____.
6. John and Volda have sold _____ house.
7. We don't know if_____ arriving today.
8. After breakfast Aaron and Mikayla put on_____ school clothes.
9. The ducks were waddling to the pond over _____.
10. I swept the yard and then I had to pick up_____ toys.

Two, to, too

Two is the number after one, e.g. one and one are two.

To means to go towards, in the direction of, e.g. I am going to Sydney.

Too means also, e.g. If your car is big enough, will you take me too? It also refers to something that is excessive, e.g. It is too hot today.

 ## Exercise W 17

Choose either 'two', 'to' or 'too' to complete each sentence:

1. We are going to Wollongong _____.

2. I thought I would take the _____ dogs.

3. It is _____ cold_____ go outside without a warm coat.

4. She will come with us _____, so be prepared.

5. After we go _____ Melbourne, we'll travel with James _____.

6. Would you allow me to come with you, _____?

7. We have _____ cats and three dogs.

8. The explorers walked _____ the North Pole.

9. We're going up the mountain and from there down _____ the river.

10. I hope you don't expect me to work _____.

Who and whom

Who and **whom** are pronouns and are used when referring to people, e.g. Who is that girl? She is a girl who goes to my school; To whom were you speaking?

'Whom' is not often used in modern speech and writing. On occasions when it appears, however it follows a preposition e.g. to whom; from whom; of whom.

Note: When you are referring to an animal or thing, use 'that' or 'which', e.g. I have a dog that is brown, or, She used her umbrella which crumpled when it hit the tree.

 ## Exercise W 18

Decide whether to use 'who' or 'whom' in the following sentences:

1. They asked to _____ I was speaking.

2. Is that the boy with _____ you went to camp?

3. _____ is he taking on his date?

4. Mum knows the lady _____ wins all the prizes.

5. He is the person _____ I wanted to see.

What and which

What and *which* can both be used to ask questions. However, 'what' is used in more general enquiries, e.g. "What film are you going to see?" whereas 'which' chooses from a limited range of alternatives, e.g. "Which film are you going to see: Star Wars or Batman?"

 ## Exercise W 19

Choose either 'what' or 'which' to fill in the sentences:

1. _____ person invented the submachine gun?

2. Do you know _____ of the three children missed school today?

3. _____ elephant is the one that has tusks?

4. I'm not sure _____ dress to choose out of all these in the shop.

5. _____ was the name of the tribe that conquered the village?

Which and that

These two pronouns are often used interchangeably, though *which* is used to introduce a general clause, e.g. His letters, which were always full of jokes, amused me.

That draws attention to something specific, e.g. I want to read the letter that amused you.

'That' is also used for animals and things, e.g. This is the pen that I write with; I have a dog that likes to chase balls.

 ## Exercise W 20

In the following sentences, decide whether it is better to use 'which' or 'that':

1. Where is the suit _____ you've decided to wear?

2. His ponies, _____ he kept in the paddock, are now missing.

3. Paul has a green car _____ he drives to university.

4. His cooking, _____ we used to enjoy every night, has not been as tasty as usual.

5. It is the sort of dress _____ I always choose to wear.

When and where

When and where cannot be used to introduce noun clauses. The sentence, "Adulthood is when a person reaches the age of 21", should read, "Adulthood is the condition of a person who reaches the age of 21".

Likewise, "A tsunami is where there is an enormous tidal wave", should read: "A tsunami occurs where there is an enormous tidal wave".

Exercise W 21

Correct the following sentences using the same construction as those above:

1. Illiteracy is when a person is unable to read or write.

2. Erosion is where wind wears the rock away.

3. A stalactite is where a rock is formed by constant water dripping on it.

4. Pollution is where the environment is spoiled by man-made waste.

5. Puberty is when a person is first able to produce offspring.

Word Usage

Better Writing

Becoming a great writer involves much more than simply knowing how to use a semicolon! Writing is an art form, and the best authors spend years honing their expressive skills to create unique works of literature that capture the imagination of readers. In this section, you'll find several ways to help engage your audience, and bring life and colour to your writing.

Alliteration

Alliteration is the repetition of a particular letter or sound at the beginning of words to produce an interesting effect, e.g. Rain's restless rage rattles repeatedly; Dewdrops dwell delicately, drawing dazzling delight.

Sometimes alliteration is used to create tongue twisters, e.g. Peter Piper picked a peck of pickled peppers; Round and round the rugged rock the ragged rascal ran.

 ### Exercise W 22

Write alliterative sentences or phrases that begin with the following words:

1. frogs
2. grandmothers
3. cars
4. whispering
5. dancers

6. balls
7. swiftly
8. dazzling
9. enormous
10. dreary

Ambiguity

Ambiguity is the presence of two or more possible meanings in a sentence, e.g. We saw her duck, or, I can't recommend this book too highly. An author may use ambiguity intentionally to convey a hidden message that may only become apparent later in the text, or to allow the reader to interpret the text in a number of ways. At other times, ambiguity should be avoided to ensure clarity.

Exercise W 23

Rearrange or expand the following ambiguous sentences so their meanings become clear:

1. I promise I'll give you a ring tomorrow.

2. A cow was found by a stream by a farmer.

3. Flying planes can be dangerous.

4. I'm glad I'm a man and so is my mother.

5. They are hunting dogs.

Clichés

A cliché is a phrase which has been used over and over again until all its freshness and originality has disappeared, e.g. stand up and be counted; in this day and age; it's driving me up the wall.

When writing, try to think of your own way of expressing something instead of relying on clichés.

Exercise W 24

Re-write the following sentences by replacing the clichés that appear in bold. e.g. He's driving me up the wall! – He's really annoying me!

1. The teacher **chewed me up**.

2. Getting into trouble **made my blood boil**.

3. My sister knows exactly how to **press my buttons**.

4. I was in class so long that **my eyes glazed over.**

5. Don't **get your nose out of shape**.

6. She likes to **toot her own horn**.

7. That was **easy as pie**.

8. That was **pretty hard to swallow**.

9. He was **grasping at straws**.

10. She was **flying by the seat of her pants**.

Overworked words

There are many words which are over-used in sentences, e.g. nice; good; got; went. Your sentences will improve if you take the time to think of words that are more specific and expressive. One way of finding more appropriate words is to make use of a thesaurus.

 ## Exercise W 25

Find a more expressive way to replace the words shown in bold in the following sentences:

1. The meat pies were **great**.
2. She **got** a prize in the competition.
3. The skaters gave a **nice** display on the ice.
4. The rotten prawns had a **bad** smell.
5. We had to sit through a **dreadful** performance.
6. I **got** a bad cold after someone sneezed on me.
7. There was a **wonderful** display of flowers in the show.
8. I had an **awful** experience at the doctor's.
9. He is a **dreadful** driver.
10. She had a **bad** knee after the hockey game

Metaphors

A metaphor is a phrase or sentence which compares two things by suggesting that something is something else, e.g. My brother *is* a monkey; His nerves *are* made of steel; That man *is* a clown.

 ## Exercise W 26

Write metaphors for the following:

1. Time
2. Life
3. Death
4. Choices
5. My mother
6. The moon
7. The glutton
8. The road
9. The house
10. My school

Similes

A simile is a figure of speech that directly compares two different things, usually by employing the words 'like' (He looks *like* his father, or, My sister is *like* a crocodile), or by using 'as' (She was *as* shaky *as* a leaf; He is *as* nasty *as* a devil.)

Other words which introduce a simile are: 'as if' and 'as though'.

 ## Exercise W 27

Write similes for the following:

1. Her eyes were as blue ...
2. He runs ...
3. He fights ...
4. My father's car races ...
5. She was shaking ...
6. Mark was driving ...
7. She walks as gracefully ...
8. He was brave ...
9. The rain falls ...
10. Exams are as difficult ...

Personification

Personification is a technique in which you make a thing, idea or an animal do something only humans can do or be, e.g. The gorilla walked *like an old man*, or, My computer *throws a fit* every time I try to use it.

 ## Exercise W 28

Use personification to complete the phrases below:

1. The thunder
2. The flowers
3. The words
4. The phone
5. The fire
6. The birds
7. The time
8. The bees
9. The wind
10. The snow

Vocabulary

Synonyms

A synonym is a word which has almost the same meaning as another word. Synonyms for 'big' include 'huge', 'gigantic' and 'immense', while words like 'evil', 'naughty' and 'disastrous' are synonyms for 'bad'.

The best place to find a synonym is in a thesaurus.

Exercise V1

Find at least three synonyms for each of the following:

1. begin
2. cheat
3. dangerous
4. dull
5. earn

6. honour
7. ignorant
8. fault
9. game
10. terror

Antonyms

An antonym is a word opposite in meaning to another, for example, hot and cold; hard and soft; abroad and home.

Sometimes an antonym can be formed by adding or changing a prefix or suffix, as can be seen in absent and present; interest and disinterest; useful and useless.

Exercise V 2

Find an antonym for each of the following:

1. accept
2. artificial
3. assemble
4. allow
5. antidote

6. always
7. ascend
8. angry
9. delicate
10. dwarf

Homophones, Homographs and Homonyms

Some words are alike in the way they sound or the way they are spelt.

Homophones are words that *sound the same* as one another, but are *spelt differently.*

doe/dough, I/eye, new/knew

Homographs are *spelt the same way*, but *sound different.*

tear/tear, bow/bow, minute/minute

Homonyms are words that have *different meanings*, but *sound the same* and are *spelt the same way.*

pen/pen, spell/spell, bark/bark

 Exercise V 3

Choose the appropriate homophone from the brackets:

1. I was wearing my (new/knew) blue jeans which I'm sure you (new/knew).

2. He didn't know (where/wear) they were going and so didn't know what to (where/wear).

3. (Two/too/to) of the students are going (two/too/to) the park (two/too/to).

4. Dad told me to come over (here/hear) and then said, "Can't you (here/hear) me?"

5. I think the answer to your question is (no/know), but I really don't (no/know).

6. (Would/wood) you prefer to live near a (would/wood) or a town?

7. I'm afraid I don't (right/write) very neatly, as I wasn't taught the (right/write) way.

8. (Which/witch) spell did the nasty (which/witch) use?

9. I didn't listen to the (whether/weather) report so I don't know (whether/weather) or not to wear a raincoat.

10. When the teacher walked (passed/past) we (passed/past) out homework notes.

Onomatopoeia

Onomatopoeia refers to words that imitate or suggest the sound of the thing they describe, e.g. bees buzz; ducks quack; horses neigh; frogs croak.

Other examples of onomatopoeia are rustle, splash, whisper, moo, twitter, hiss, clang, croak, tick tock, murmur and baa.

Exercise V 4

Think of at least two words that would go with the following.

1. beep
2. clatter
3. drip
4. mumble
5. sizzle

6. rattle
7. whizz
8. jangle
9. knock
10. pop

Suffixes

Suffixes are attached to the *end* of words to change their meaning, e.g. use + suffix 'full' = useful (note that you drop the 'l' in 'full'); assist + suffix 'ance' = assistance; problem + suffix 'atic' = problematic.

Here is a list of some other suffixes:

-able	-ate	-eer	-ese	-gon	-ide	-ish	-less	-oid	-ship	-woman
-age	-atic	-en	-ess	-hood	-ie	-ism	-let	-or	-some	-y
-aholic	-ation	-ence	-est	-ian	-ify	-ist	-logy	-ory	-th	
-al	-ary	-ency	-ette	-ible	-ine	-ite	-ly	-phile	-tion	
-an	-cide	-ent	-fold	-ic	-ing	-it	-man	-phobia	-ty	
-ance	-cy	-er	-ful	-ical	-ion	-ity	-ment	-proof	-ward	
-ancy	-ed	-ery	-fy	-ice	-ious	-ive	-most	-ry	-ways	
-ant	-ee	-es	-gate	-ics	-ise	-ise	-ness	-s	-wise	

 Exercise V 5

Use the suffixes above to change the meaning of the following words:

1. weather
2. kind
3. human
4. flexible
5. digest

6. hope
7. equal
8. friend
9. meet
10. dust

Prefixes

Prefixes are attached to the *beginning* of words to change their meaning, e.g. cycle + prefix 'bi' = bicycle; metre + prefix 'centi' = centimetre; biography + prefix 'auto' = autobiography.

Here is a list of some other prefixes:

a-	col-	dia-	for-	hyper-	mal-	ob-	post-	sex-	turbo-
aero-	com-	digi-	fore-	hypo-	mega-	octa-	pre-	socio-	ultra-
ambi-	cor-	dys-	geo-	ig-	meta-	octo-	pro-	sub-	un-
anti-	con-	e-	grand-	il-	micro-	omni-	pseudo-	super-	under-
astro-	contra-	eco-	great-	im-	mid-	ortho-	psycho-	sym-	uni-
audio-	counter-	electro-	hect-	in-	milli-	out-	quad-	syn-	vice-
be-	cyber-	em-	hector-	ir-	mis-	over-	quin-	techno-	video-
bi-	de-	en-	hemi-	infra-	mono-	penta-	re-	tele-	
biblio-	deca-	equip-	hepta-	inter-	multi-	peri-	retro-	theo-	
bio-	deci-	Euro-	hexa-	intra-	neo-	photo-	self-	thermal-	
by-	demi-	ex-	homo-	kilo-	neuro-	physio-	semi-	trans-	
chron-	di-	extra-	hydro	macro-	non-	poly-	sept-	tri-	

 Exercise V 6

Use prefixes above to change the meaning of the following words:

1. red
2. tasking
3. grams
4. help
5. noon
6. transparent
7. cycle
8. angle
9. space
10. counter

Animals and their babies

Name of creature	Male	Female	Young
cat	tomcat	queen	kitten
horse	stallion	mare	foal
bear	bear	she-bear	cub
goat	billy-goat	nanny-goat	kid
deer	buck	doe	fawn
pig	boar	sow	piglet
hare	buck	doe	leveret
rabbit	buck	doe	rack
cattle	bull	cow	calf
elephant	bull	cow	calf
seal	bull	cow	calf
whale	bull	cow	calf
dog	dog	bitch	pup, puppy
fox	dog	vixen	cub
donkey	donkey	mare	foal
lion	lion	lioness	cub
sheep	ram	ewe	lamb
tiger	tiger	tigress	cub
wolf	wolf	she-wolf	cub
swan	cob	pen	cygnet
fowl	cock	hen	chicken
pigeon	cock	hen	squab
duck	drake	duck	duckling

continued...

continued...

Name of creature	Male	Female	Young
eagle	eagle	eagle	eaglet
goose	gander	goose	gosling
owl	owl	owl	owlet
peafowl	peacock	peahen	peachick

Name of creature	Young
ant, bee, beetle, wasp	grub
butterfly, moth	caterpillar
cockroach	nymph
eel	elver
fly	maggot
frog, toad	tadpole
salmon	parr
trout	fry

 Exercise V 7

What do you call the young of the following?

1. swan
2. hare
3. duck
4. salmon
5. people

6. cockroach
7. wasp
8. eagle
9. pigeon
10. peafowl

Homes of creatures

Creature	Home	Creature	Home
fowl	coop	wasp	nest
cow	byre, pen	pigeon	dove-cot
hare	form	beaver, otter	lodge
rabbit (tame)	hutch	rabbit (wild)	warren
sheep	pen, fold	tiger	lair
ape	tree-nest	eagle	eyrie
mole	fortress	squirrel	drey
bear	den	dog	kennel

 Exercise V 8

What do you call the homes of the following?

1. snail
2. spider
3. pigeon
4. ant
5. turtle
6. fowl
7. hare
8. mole
9. bee
10. horse

People's occupations

An **anthropologist** studies human beings

A **biologist** studies living things

A **botanist** studies plants and trees

A **cobbler** mends shoes

A **confectioner** makes or sells cakes, sweets, pastries, etc

An **economist** studies about the science of production and distribution of goods

A **draper** sells cloth and articles of clothing

An **entomologist** studies insects

An **etymologist** studies the origin and history of words

A **funambulist** (or tight-rope walker) walks on ropes

A **goldsmith** makes and sells gold articles

A **hawker** goes from place to place to sell things

A **lapidist** cuts, polishes, or engraves precious stones or gems

A **lexicographer** compiles a dictionary

A **mason** does stone-work for buildings

A **numismatist** collects or is an expert on coins

A **philologist** studies the nature and development of language

A **pathologist** studies diseases

A **philatelist** collects stamps

A **poulterer** sells fowls, ducks, geese, etc

A **porter** carries luggage at an airport, railway station, etc

A **retailer** sells goods in small quantities

A **semanticist** studies the changes in the meanings of words

A **sociologist** studies the nature and growth of society

A **stenographer** can write dictation in shorthand

A **wholesaler** sells goods in large quantities

Exercise V 9

What do you call the following people?

1. Someone who makes furniture

2. Someone who draws pictures very well

3. Someone who designs buildings

4. Someone who studies the sun, moon, planets and stars

5. Someone who studies insects

6. Someone who studies the nature and development of language

7. Someone who draws plans for a building

8. Someone who writes plays or dramas

9. Someone who improves and prepares a book for printing

10. Someone who sends goods to a foreign country.

Receptacles

A receptacle is a container or holder in which things may be put away safely or out of sight. A cabinet, for example, is a piece of furniture in which interesting and beautiful things are kept for show.

Name of receptacle	Description
caddy	a small box for tea
casket	a small beautiful box for jewels
canister	a small contained for tea, coffee, etc
cauldron	a large pot for cooking or boiling
cistern	a water-tank in a building
creel	a basket for carrying fish
cruet	a small glass bottle for oil, vinegar, sauce etc
holster	a leather case for a pistol
kitbag	a canvas bag in which a soldier or sailor keeps their belongings
pouch	a small bag or purse carried in the pocket on one's belt
phial, vial	a small glass bottle for holding perfume, medicine, etc
pitcher	a large jug or container for holding and pouring out liquids

continued...

continued...

portmanteau	a travelling trunk or case
portfolio	a leather handbag for carrying documents, writing materials, drawings, etc
quiver	a case to carry darts or arrows
salver	a small metal tray for letters, etc
scabbard, sheath	a case for a sword, dagger, etc
scuttle	a bucket or box for coal, kept near a fire
shrine	a place where sacred things are kept
till	a drawer in a shop for keeping money
trough	a long narrow container for holding food or water for animals, e.g. horse, cow
vault	an underground room for valuables, usually in a bank

✏ Exercise V 10

What is the name given to the following receptacles?

1. A leather bag for documents such as important letters

2. A large pot used for boiling food

3. A vase for holding the ashes of the dead

4. A piece of furniture for holding personal belongings, eg clothes, tools

5. A small cupboard with a lock used for keeping books, etc

6. A leather bag for carrying documents

7. A case for carrying arrows

8. A light travelling case for clothes and other belongings

9. A tank for storing petrol

10. A bottle for carrying drinks in one's pocket

Places

An **abattoir or slaughterhouse** is where sheep, cattle, etc are slaughtered

An **auditorium** is a building in which an audience sits

A **boutique** is a small shop selling women's clothes and accessories, etc

A **crematorium** is a place or building for the burning of corpses

A **dispensary** is a place (eg a pharmacy or hospital) where medicine is prepared

An **emporium** is a shop selling a wide variety of goods

A **reservoir** is an artificial lake where water is stored for the public

A **mosque** is a Muslim place of worship

A **temple** is a Hindu or Buddhist place of worship

A **synagogue** is a Jewish place of worship

An **infirmary** is a place in which the sick or injured are nursed

A **confectionery** is a shop where cakes, pies and other sweets are sold

A **hangar** is a shed which houses aeroplanes

A **quarry** is a place where stone, etc. is excavated for the purpose of building houses, etc

A **shipyard** is a place where ships are built or repaired

An **apiary** is a place where bees are kept

An **archive** is a place where public records are kept

An **aviary** is a place where birds are kept

A **distillery** is a place where strong alcoholic drinks (eg whisky) are made

A **foundry** is a place where metal, glass etc are melted and moulded

A **granary** is a building where grain is stored

A **mortuary** is a place where dead people are kept before burial (eg in a funeral parlour or hospital)

A **reformatory** is an institution where young law-breakers are sent to be trained as good citizens

A **sanatorium** is a hospital where the sick are looked after

A t**annery** is a place where animal skins are tanned

Exercise V 11

What do you call the following places?

1. A room used for cooking

2. A large field for aeroplanes

3. A place for burying the dead

4. A shop selling a variety of goods

5. An artificial lake where water is stored for the public

6. A Christian place of worship

7. A place for shelter of ships

8. A narrow passage between buildings

9. A plot of land on which fruit trees are grown

10. A place where ships are built or repaired

Collective nouns

An **army** of soldiers; ants

A **band** of musicians; robbers

A **bevy** of quails; beauties

A **brood** of chickens

A **class** of scholars; students

A **colony** of gulls

A **company** of actors; soldiers

A **compendium** of games

A **congregation** of worshippers

A **constellation** (or **galaxy**) of stars

A **drove** of cattle

A **dynasty** of kings

A **flight** of doves; swallows

continued...

continued...

A **gaggle** of geese

A **garland** (or **bunch**) of flowers

A **litter** of piglets; puppies; kittens

A **menagerie** (or **zoo**) of wild animals

A **murder** of crows

A **regiment** of soldiers

A **staff** of servants; employees; teachers

A **stud** of horses

A **tribe** of goats; natives

A **troop** of lions; monkeys; scouts

A **tuft** of hair; grass

A **wad** of notes

 Exercise V 12

What are the collective nouns for the following?

1. porpoises

2. thieves

3. geese

4. singers

5. flies

6. monkeys

7. chickens

8. cubs

9. people

10. sailors

11. angels

12. kittens

13. policemen

14. rioters

15. servants

16. dancers

17. hair

18. furniture

19. stars

20. flowers

Forming nouns

Nouns can be formed from adjectives, e.g. bitter (adj), bitterness (n); active (adj), activity (n); brave (adj), bravery (noun).

Nouns can also be formed from verbs, e.g. ascend (vb), ascent (n); grow (vb), growth (n); attend (vb), attendance (n).

You can change adjectives and verbs into nouns by:
- Adding ness, e.g. sad, sadness; bitter, bitterness
- Adding "ty", e.g. certain, certainty; beautiful, beauty
- Adding "ety", e.g. anxious, anxiety; safe, safety
- Adding "ity", e.g. superior, superiority; actual, actuality
- Adding "y", e.g. enquire, enquiry; register, registry
- Adding "cy", e.g. efficient, efficiency; decent, decency
- Adding "ry", e.g. rival, rivalry; brave, bravery;
- Adding "nce", e.g. absent, absence; present, presence
- Adding "t", e.g. hot, heat; think, thought
- Adding "th", e.g. deep, depth; long, length
- Adding "ment", e.g. enlarge, enlargement; abandon, abandonment
- Adding "tion", e.g. add, addition; dictate; dictation
- Adding "sion", e.g. permit, permission; omit, omission
- Adding "ship", e.g. owner, ownership; friend, friendship
- Adding "hood", e.g. child, childhood; neighbour, neighbourhood
- Adding 'dom', e.g. king, kingdom; serf, serfdom
- Adding 'ism', e.g. social, socialism; hero, heroism
- Adding 'ice', e.g. advise, advice; practise, practice

Note: Some nouns and verbs do not change, e.g. fight can be both a noun and verb; abuse can be both a noun and verb. Other words which do not change include:

walk	delight	drop	damage	quarrel
need	sleep	decay	parade	barricade
stop	drop	pull	dream	quarrel

Exercise V 13

Change the following words into nouns:

1. favour
2. free
3. create
4. argue
5. encourage
6. obedient
7. responsible
8. mock
9. blunt
10. extreme

Forming verbs

Nouns and adjectives can be formed into verbs by:

- Beginning with 'en': courage, encourage; danger, endanger
- Beginning with 'dis': close, disclose; trust, distrust
- Beginning with 'mis': rule, misrule; guide, misguide
- Ending with 'en': sad, sadden; bright, brighten
- Ending in 'ise': memory, memorise; economy, economise
- Ending in 'ify': notice, notify; beautiful, beautify
- Ending in 'ate': vegetation, vegetate; education, educate
- Ending in 'ade': persuasion, persuade; evasion, evade
- Ending in 'ide': decision, decide; collision, collide

Other examples:

bath, bathe	breath, breathe	bitter, embitter	company, accompany
custom, customise	food, feed	friend, befriend	full, fill
head, behead	prison, imprison	safe, save	

Exercise V 14

Change the following words into verbs:

1. poverty
2. admission
3. choice
4. exploration
5. concealment
6. growth
7. fluency
8. purity
9. cloud
10. truth

Forming adjectives

Nouns and verbs can be formed into adjectives by:

- Ending in 'ous', e.g. adventure, adventurous; mischief, mischievous
- Ending in 'y', e.g. silver, silvery; taste, tasty
- Ending in 'ly', e.g. beast, beastly; cowardice, cowardly
- Ending in 'al', e.g. crime, criminal; accident, accidental
- Ending in 'ar', e.g. circle, circular; single, singular
- Ending in 'ful', e.g. beauty, beautiful; youth, youthful
- Ending in 'less', e.g. use, useless; sense, senseless
- Ending in 'able', e.g. advise, advisable; agree, agreeable
- Ending in 'ible', e.g. terror, terrible; horror, horrible
- Ending in 'ic', e.g. volcano, volcanic; comedy, comic
- Ending in 'ish', e.g. Britain, British; self, selfish
- Ending in 'ive', e.g. indicate, indicative; inform, informative

Other examples:

| favour, favourite | imagine, imaginary | north, northern | please, pleasant |
| quarrel, quarrelsome | slip, slippery | trouble, troublesome; | war, warlike |

Exercise V 15

Change the following words into adjectives:

1. learn
2. satisfy
3. notice
4. sell
5. people

6. spirit
7. originate
8. vision
9. centre
10. fog

Exercises
to test yourself

Grammar

Types of Nouns

✎ Exercise GT 1

State whether the nouns below are common, proper, collective or abstract:

1. petunias _____
2. love _____
3. Samuel _____
4. litter _____
5. energy _____

6. hatred _____
7. avenue _____
8. Jones _____
9. mass _____
10. flock _____

Singular

✎ Exercise GT 2

Write the singular form of the following words:

1. crises _____
2. ellipses _____
3. plural _____
4. sheep _____
5. knives _____

6. beaux _____
7. people _____
8. citizens _____
9. traumata _____
10. stimuli _____

Plurals

✎ Exercise GT 3

Write the plural form of the following words:

1. parenthesis _____
2. radius _____
3. logo _____
4. monsieur _____
5. baggage _____
6. mother-in-law _____
7. staff _____

8. witch _____
9. glory _____
10. dynamo _____
11. echo _____
12. chassis _____
13. nucleus _____
14. shelf _____

REPRODUCIBLE

Grammar

Pronouns

✎ Exercise GT

Write a sentence for each of the following kinds of pronouns:

1. *Personal pronoun* _____

   _____

2. *Reflexive pronouns* _____

   _____

3. *Relative pronouns* _____

   _____

4. *Interrogative pronouns* _____

   _____

5. *Demonstrative pronouns* _____

   _____

6. *Indefinite pronouns*_____

   _____

Prepositions

✎ Exercise GT 5

Use the correct preposition in the spaces:

1. We offered our **congratulations** to the couple _____ getting engaged.

2. Wesley was **accompanied** _____ his best friend.

3. Dad was **pleased** _____ my high scores in the test.

4. I don't like people who **profit** _____ over-taxing customers.

5. My brother is pleased to be **independent** _____ our parents.

6. The land lies **adjacent** _____ the house.

7. When you were small, did you **succeed** _____ school?

8. Mabel is always **boasting** _____ her garden display.

9. The lawn was **covered** _____ leaves.

REPRODUCIBLE

Grammar

Adjectives

✎ Exercise GT 6

List the adjectives in the following sentences and identify what type of adjective they are:

1. Nicole scored twenty runs in the cricket game. _____
   _____

2. The terrible twins Steve and Jett never clean their room. _____
   _____

3. Which of the dogs would you like: the one with the wiggly tail or the one with sad eyes? _____
   _____

4. Here comes that silly woman who asks many questions. _____
   _____

5. The famous chef showed everyone how to make his delicious pumpkin soup _____
   _____

Making Comparisons

✎ Exercise GT 7

Write the comparative and superlative forms of the following adjectives:

1. Wise _____
2. Frugal _____
3. Merry _____
4. Short _____
5. Beautiful _____

6. Angry _____
7. Colourful _____
8. Popular _____
9. Steep _____
10. Pleasant _____

Grammar

Verbs

✎ Exercise GT 8

Write three verbs to describe the following, e.g. Horse: Gallops, Trots:

1. Burglar: _____ , _____ , _____
2. Drunk: _____ , _____ , _____
3. Old person: _____ , _____ , _____
4. Mice: _____ , _____ , _____
5. Skater: _____ , _____ , _____
6. Waves: _____ , _____ , _____
7. Flowers: _____ , _____ , _____
8. Dog: _____ , _____ , _____
9. Soldier: _____ , _____ , _____
10. Queen: _____ , _____ , _____

Tenses

✎ Exercise GT 9

Identify the tense in the space next to each sentence:

1. From one end of the pool I swim leisurely. _____
2. I've had enough of this game: I'm going home! _____
3. A box of chocolates is what I'll buy Mum for Mother's Day. _____
4. She is a person I can trust._____
5. When we went to Melbourne, we saw where Ned Kelly was hung. _____
6. I once thought that watermelons grew on trees! _____
7. I was going to the concert, but I had to turn back. _____
8. My friends are all jealous of my new car. _____
9. I have had an accident, last night, so I was late to the party. _____
10. How many times have you visited Europe? _____

Grammar

Auxiliary verbs

 **Exercise GT 10**

- _____
- _____
- _____
- _____
- _____
- _____
- _____
- _____

- _____
- _____
- _____
- _____
- _____
- _____
- _____
- _____

- _____
- _____
- _____
- _____
- _____
- _____
- _____
- _____

There are 25 auxiliary verbs. Write down as many as you can remember.

Participles

 **Exercise GT 11**

Underline the participles in the following sentences:

1. The man is approaching the station where a train is waiting.

2. Running around the oval are thirteen panting athletes.

3. The presenter has talked for three boring hours.

4. We have had enough of his endless speech.

5. Joel is a comedian, playing to an audience too afraid to laugh.

6. Lying on the grass, Anthony and Kelly saw a shooting star.

7. Visibly shaken, the woman walked away from the wrecked car.

8. I could tell someone was home because the chimney was smoking.

REPRODUCIBLE

Grammar

Gerunds

✎ Exercise GT 12

Create sentences by changing the following verbs into gerunds:

1. sneeze _____

_____

2. cook: _____

_____

3. dance _____

_____

4. read _____

_____

5. do _____

_____

Adverbs

✎ Exercise GT 13

Underline the adverbs in the following sentences:

1. He has almost managed to perform weekly for two months now.
2. He put the bags outside under the apple tree.
3. Every day I swim fast to warm myself up in the cold pool.
4. Never have I seen anyone walk like that!
5. My grandfather is too old to walk everywhere now.
6. The pie I made yesterday was surprisingly good.
7. I drove across the country to deliver the car to the new owner.
8. The Christmas tree was very tall, and illuminated brilliantly.
9. She is almost always cheerful.
10. I wanted a higher score on the exam, but I didn't work hard enough.

REPRODUCIBLE

Grammar

Sentences

✎ Exercise GT 14

Rewrite the following sentences using correct punctuation, then decide whether they are statements, questions, commands or exclamations:

1. you should check your weight after eating all that fatty food _____

   _____

2. what an amazing person you are _____

   _____

3. what are you doing with that handgun _____

   _____

4. neither the cow nor the horse was found _____

   _____

5. were you part of the crowd that attended the rock concert _____

   _____

6. how many times have I told you not to do that _____

   _____

7. wow, I didn't know you could do that _____

   _____

8. milly has three sisters – Tilly, Jilly and Petunia _____

   _____

9. do it right now _____

   _____

10. i suppose you'll never forgive me; is that right _____

    _____

REPRODUCIBLE

Grammar

Subject

✎ Exercise GT 15

Underline the subjects in the following sentences:

1. A large car stopped in front of our house.

2. His constant drumming annoyed the neighbours.

3. Whom to hire is a difficult question.

4. "I love you", is what the man said to his fiancé.

5. It was a gift from him to them.

6. Green is my favourite colour.

7. A Christmas card from Aunt Judy arrived in the mail.

8. The plumber fixed the pipes under the sink.

Object

Underline the objects in the following sentences:

✎ Exercise GT 16

1. Give the football to me, not him.

2. In the jungle, lions hunt for prey.

3. After the final song, the drummer hurled his sticks at the crowd.

4. Marcus stunned the giraffe with a radar gun.

5. Heaping his plate with fried chicken, Dad winked at the cook.

6. Mike ran past the group of people who were jogging.

7. Grandad gave me the cricket bat he used as a kid.

8. Rachel won a prize at the science fair.

Grammar

Phrases

✎ **Exercise GT 17**

Insert phrases in the following sentences:

1. He slipped the envelope _____ and then left _____.

2. Putting the slipper _____ he hobbled _____ .

3. She's a singer _____ who always pleases her audiences.

4. _____ sits a fat, white cat.

5. Can you please put string _____ and then tie the knot?

6. Our class obtained the first three places _____

7. Do you know the song _____ ?

8. She helps me _____

9. Don't put it _____ !

10. _____ jumped the cow, followed by the dog.

Clauses

✎ **Exercise GT 18**

Underline the clauses in the following sentences:

1. You'll be much happier when the trouble passes.

2. Whenever lazy students whine, my teacher laughs.

3. Tony ran for the paper towels as cola spilled over the table.

4. Because my dog loves pizza crusts, he never barks at the deliveryman.

5. A person who eats too many sugary foods will soon develop rotten teeth.

6. You really do not want to know what Aunt Nancy adds to her stew.

7. Bill blushed because Di smiled at him.

8. We all cheered when the football team scored a goal.

9. I don't like people who lie and cheat.

10. My sister isn't very popular because she gossips too much.

REPRODUCIBLE

Grammar

Conjunctions

✎ Exercise GT 19

Use conjunctions to join the following sentences:

1. We stayed indoors. It was raining. _____

_____

_____

2. I'm wearing a woolly jumper. The temperature is in the high thirties. ____

_____

_____

3. We shopped at the supermarket. We went home. _____

_____

_____

4. He ran. He jumped. He whooped with joy. _____

_____

_____

5. I was feeling tired. I went home. _____

_____

_____

6. We looked after Mimi's dog. Mimi was overseas. _____

_____

_____

7. Bob was tired. He was hungry. He cooked dinner and went to bed. _____

_____

_____

8. Jack went to bed. So did Judy. _____

_____

_____

9. He washed the dishes. I dried them. _____

_____

_____

10. Rick started up the car's engine. At the same time Jack listened for the noise. _____

_____

_____

REPRODUCIBLE

Grammar

Voice

✎ Exercise GT 20

Decide whether the sentences below are in the active or passive voice, then re-write them in the opposite voice:

The man was arrested by the civilian. (Active/Passive)

_____

_____

1. Maud lifted the revolver and shot the trespasser. (Active/Passive)

_____

_____

2. Scientists have found evidence of ice on Mars. (Active/Passive)

_____

_____

3. Thieves are stealing diamonds from the shop. (Active/Passive)

_____

_____

4. A letter was delivered by the postman to Mr Jones. (Active/Passive)

_____

_____

5. The group will present the report next week. (Active/Passive)

_____

_____

6. The teacher asked many difficult questions. (Active/Passive)

_____

_____

7. My bike and helmet were stolen by some bullies. (Active/Passive)

_____

_____

8. Most of the class is reading the book. (Active/Passive)

_____

_____

9. I accidently left the stove on when I left the house. (Active/Passive)

_____

_____

REPRODUCIBLE

Punctuation

Capital letters

✎ Exercise PT 1

Write the following sentences and insert any missing capital letters and other punctuation:

1. when we went to canberra we drove over lake burley griffin and visited the national war memorial

2. do you know that my father is sir william condon

3. susie and i live in mount street but next may we are moving to broadway lane

4. last tuesday I visited dr marshall for a check up

5. her majesty queen elizabeth II lives in buckingham palace in london

Full stops and commas

✎ Exercise PT 2

In the following sentences, insert the missing full stops and commas:

1. I swept the yard weeded the garden and then I had to cook dinner for Jim Danny and John
2. He bought a fast green car
3. My brother Larry who is usually a healthy man now has a fever
4. It is a great honour to introduce my friends Ann and Julie
5. He asked question after question and then he paused saying "I think you have the flu".
6. Mum always puts fruit into my lunchbox my favourites are apples bannanas and pears
7. The man playing blackjack was dealt a three a two and a queen

REPRODUCIBLE

Punctuation

Brackets and dashes

✎ Exercise PT 3

Rewrite the following sentences, inserting the missing brackets or dashes and other necessary punctuation:

1. the second world war 1939 1945 involved many nations including england and germany _____

_____

2. it was a tough match to win victorian players are rough _____

_____

3. vicki wore a dress a prized possession to the ball _____

_____

4. the woman was lying on the bed dead _____

_____

5. she assembled all the ingredients flour margarine eggs sugar and sultanas and started making the cake _____

_____

6. cheval place in chester is where youll find the princess theatre _____

_____

Hyphens

✎ Exercise PT 4

Insert the missing hyphens in the following sentences:

1. Jerry is so self reliant, he works non stop from morning to night in the multi storeyed office block.
2. While out walking, I collected grass seeds in my hiking boots.
3. As I made too many errors, I resigned the letter to impress my difficult to please boss.
4. Mum says my sister's boy friend is a good for nothing who ought to get himself a decent job.
5. We bought home made marmalade from a middle aged woman at the fete.

REPRODUCIBLE

Punctuation

Colons and semicolons

✎ Exercise PT 5

Insert the missing colons or semicolons below, as well as any other necessary punctuation.

1. This year I am studying these subjects english biology art and history
2. Jack strolled along the beach picking up shells then he found a prize piece of driftwood
3. Jim locked himself in his room his team had lost the cricket match.
4. My mother taught me two golden rules I was to do my best and always tell the truth
5. The rocket rose it twisted in the air it suddenly burst into flames.

Apostrophes

✎ Exercise PT 6

In the following sentences insert the missing apostrophes:

1. Its time we were all in bed, seeing as shes asked us five times already.
2. Julia and Mattys house is built next to Robs.
3. Can you collect its blanket and give it to the neighbours son Alex?
4. I couldnt have cared less about homework, but my two friends efforts made me change my mind.
5. Jaggers and McCartneys songwriting skills were distinct and different.

Ellipses

✎ Exercise PT 7

Rewrite the following sentences, inserting the missing ellipses:

1. What the is going on? _____
2. I put it somewhere now where was it? _____
3. I was going to but I forget what it was I was going to do. _____
4. look there can you see it? _____
5. it's a monstrous _____

REPRODUCIBLE

Punctuation

Quotation marks

✎ Exercise PT 8

Rewrite the following passage, inserting the missing quotation marks and other necessary punctuation. Remember to include paragraph spaces.

Im pregnant said mum I stared at her i couldnt believe what she had said youre what mum picked up her cup of tea she took a sip im going to have a baby was I hearing right you can't have a baby i said mum and dad smiled at one another like id said something really funny oh and why not said mum youre too old im only thirty two not too old but i didn't know what else to say

----

Punctuation

Punctuation

✎ Exercise PT 9

Rewrite the following passage, inserting capital letters, full stops, commas, question marks and anything else you think necessary:

hes too skinny the stout indian with the long black moustache looked at amin the four year old boy in front of him but hes strong for his age said amins father sa'id if you give him good food as you promised he will surely fatten up amin's stomach ached but he wasn't worried about that his stomach often ached from lack of food what most ached at that moment was his heart all through the night just past he had listened to his parents talking his mother had cried again and again she and his father talked about him their second-youngest son papa talked about indenturing him to the indian amin didn't understand the word indentured but he knew that his father wanted to sell him to the indian once before now the indian had come to his village he had bought four children including amins older sister zarina and his brother suleiman four hundred rupees the indian said that's all your skinny son is worth four hundred rupees will only feed my family for one week said sa'id please kind sir could you make his price one thousand rupees the Indian laughed loud and long to amin he sounded like a hyena surely you jest nine hundred i will give you five hundred the haggling went on and on

_____

_____

_____

_____

_____

_____

_____

_____

_____

_____

_____

_____

_____

_____

REPRODUCIBLE

Word Usage

✎ Exercise WT 1

Choose the correct word from the brackets in the following sentences:

1. Share the sweets (among/between) the five children, please.

2. (Can/May) I borrow your lawn-mower?

3. There are (less/fewer) people here than I thought there might be.

4. Shane is the boy (who/whom) we were discussing last night.

5. Penny owns (a/the) dog you can see over there.

6. Matty found (a/an) orange-coloured cat in the lane.

7. Have you (bought/brought) some food along today to share with us all?

8. He has (less/fewer) to worry about than you have.

9. Are you going to (lay/lie) down and have a nap?

10. Please don't (bring/take) that old thing to the party tomorrow.

✎ Exercise WT 2

Choose the correct word from the brackets in the following sentences:

1. She is the person (who/whom) forgot her permission note.

2. I don't know her very (good/well).

3. (Lay/Lie) that book on the desk, please.

4. Hal had (laid/lain) his belongings on the bed.

5. He (lied/laid) about where he was that day.

6. When I go to camp, what should I (bring/take)?

7. I can't see (who/whom) is over there.

8. Please (lend/loan) me your favourite book.

9. I (shall/will) depart by train in the morning.

10. They (shall/will) go or there will be trouble.

REPRODUCIBLE

Word Usage

✎ Exercise WT 3

Choose the correct word from the brackets in the following sentences:

1. The rules take (affect/effect) straight away.

2. How did it (effect/affect) you having a stranger in your home?

3. (Bring/Take) that mess away from here!

4. (May/Can) you fix the broken pipe?

5. Sir, (may/can) I go to the toilet, please?

6. Neither Rob nor (I/me) have been to the opera.

7. She did (good/well) in the yearly exams.

8. Her drawings, (which/that) were excellent, were chosen for the display.

9. Give me the clothes (that/which) need ironing.

10. Emily has a new baby (that/which/who) is named Noah.

✎ Exercise WT 4

Choose the correct word from the brackets in the following sentences:

1. (What/Which) book are you going to read next?

2. (They're/There/Their) stories didn't tally, so I knew they were (laying/lying).

3. Put the machine over (they're/there/their) and leave it to me to fix it.

4. The detective examined (they're/there/their) clothes for evidence.

5. Will you please (lend/loan) me your (two/to/too) books?

6. Are you going (two/to/too) the cinema with those (two/to/too)?

7. She is (two/to/too) dishonest for me to trust her.

8. He hasn't (anything/nothing) to say about the accident.

9. Matty (can't/can) hardly wait until his birthday.

10. We all (swum/swam) at the beach yesterday.

REPRODUCIBLE

Word Usage

✎ Exercise WT 5

Choose the correct word from the brackets in the following sentences:

1. The crowd (was/were) a huge one – over three thousand people.

2. The crowd of three thousand (is/are) behaving badly.

3. Three thousand people (is/are) behaving badly.

4. Since the committee is in charge, (it/they) has the final decision.

5. Neither the dogs nor the cat (was/were) found to have the disease.

6. A pair of scissors (was/were) used.

7. In the news (is/are) many stories about car accidents.

8. Fifty head of cattle (are/is) being sold tomorrow at the auction.

9. Thanks was given to the woman who (has/had) organised the event.

10. This kind of apple (are/is) delicious.

✎ Exercise WT 6

Choose the correct word from the brackets in the following sentences:

1. The (younger/youngest) of the three girls is called Sally.

2. These kinds of mistakes (is/are) very costly.

3. Of the four children, the (elder/eldest) is the most educated.

4. This year there were (less/fewer) prizes.

5. Every cow and bull (was/were) sold.

6. The fastest in the world, the aeroplane (is/are) now being mass produced.

7. My dog was the (more/most) valuable in the show.

8. Jimmy is the (taller/tallest) boy in the class.

9. If he and (I/me) ever meet, we're sure to like one another.

10. (Who/whom) did you see at the movies?

REPRODUCIBLE

Word Usage

✎ Exercise WT 7

Choose the correct word in brackets in the following sentences:

1. I am not sure if either of the two girls (are/is) to come with us.

2. Neither the men nor the woman (are/is) sitting on the jury.

3. I wish that my neighbour would stop playing that (continuous/continual) music all night.

4. I don't care about music one way or another; I'm really (disinterested/uninterested).

5. Robin was (disinterested/uninterested) in her mother's new dress.

6. The train was (stationary/stationery), waiting for passengers.

7. I must (of/have) lost my necklace when I was at your place.

8. We walked (about/around) the property looking for the missing horses.

9. The boy I saw must have been (about/around) seven years old.

10. Lucy took out her (stationary/stationery) and began writing a letter to her grandmother.

✎ Exercise WT 8

Choose the correct word in brackets in the following sentences:

1. Harry and (I/me) are going shopping.

2. Are you going to give the ball to Tom or to (I/me)?

3. He gave Nanette and (I/me) the apples.

4. There are no secrets between you and (I/me).

5. He didn't hide from Peter; he hid from (I/me).

REPRODUCIBLE

Word Usage

Clichés

✎ Exercise WT 9

Replace the highlighted clichés with your own words:

1. **Live and learn**; that's what my mother always told me. _____
   _____

2. You'll never get anywhere in life if you **don't stay the course**. _____
   _____

3. People often say, "**What goes around comes around**." _____
   _____

4. He says that his children are always **biting the hand that feeds them.** ____
   _____

5. That girl really **gets under my skin**! _____
   _____

6. She's **no spring chicken**! _____
   _____

Alliteration

✎ Exercise WT 10

Write alliterative sentences or phrases that begin with the following words

1. Trains _____
2. Ducks _____
3. Ten _____
4. Poor _____
5. Marching _____
6. Lucky _____
7. Gavin _____
8. More _____

REPRODUCIBLE

Word Usage

Similes and Metaphors

✎ Exercise WT 11

Decide whether the following sentences contain similes or metaphors.

1. He was as hungry as a horse   _____

2. The sunshine felt like a warm blanket.   _____

3. The tightrope walker must have nerves of steel.   _____

4. Like a silent thief, the dog crept into the kitchen.   _____

5. My mind buzzed with creative ideas.   _____

6. The house was as quiet as a tomb.   _____

7. The cold cut through me like a dagger.   _____

8. His news was met with an avalanche of questions. _____

9. Her love melted his frozen heart.   _____

10. Jenny's daughter is a little angel.   _____

Personification

✎ Exercise WT 12

Use the following words to create examples of personification:

1. Smile _____

_____

2. Beg _____

_____

3. Angry _____

_____

4. Dance _____

_____

5. Play _____

_____

REPRODUCIBLE

Word Usage

Ambiguity

✎ Exercise WT 13

Rewrite the following ambiguous sentences so that their meaning becomes clear.

1. I noticed a kangaroo catching the bus this morning _____
    _____

2. She bought a sofa from the man with wobbly legs. _____
    _____

3. He wore a hat on his head made of felt. _____
    _____

4. Dad announced that he was building a factory after breakfast. _____
    _____

5. We sang a tune in the concert about a man who fell in love. _____
    _____

6. The lady hit the man with an umbrella. _____
    _____

7. Toni gave her cat food. _____

8. _____

9. The school is looking for French, German and Japanese teachers. _____
    _____

10. Did you see the girl with the telescope? _____
    _____

11. The chicken is ready to eat. _____
    _____

12. I looked at the dog with one eye. _____
    _____

13. The teacher said on Monday he would test his students. _____
    _____

REPRODUCIBLE

Word Usage

Overworked Words

✎ Exercise WT 14

Rewrite each sentence below, replacing the following highlighted words with stronger, more appropriate words:

1. We ate a **nice** pot roast. _____

   _____

2. Look at what I **got** from my best friend! _____

   _____

3. It's a **lovely** necklace. _____

   _____

4. You look so **pretty** in that dress. _____

   _____

5. We **went** to Canada by plane and then by train. _____

   _____

6. I had a **terrible** time last night at the haunted house. _____

   _____

7. My brother's behaviour is so **bad**. _____

   _____

8. I always have a **good** time at Adventure World. _____

   _____

9. My aunt **got** the flu from her cat. _____

   _____

10. He went **well** in his exams. _____

    _____

11. The fireworks were **awesome**. _____

    _____

12. She is such a **good** girl to take her little brother to the movies. _____

    _____

REPRODUCIBLE

Vocabulary

Synonyms

✎ Exercise VT 1

Write two synonyms for each of the following words:

1. abandon   _____   _____
2. profit   _____   _____
3. coarse   _____   _____
4. remedy   _____   _____
5. exterior   _____   _____
6. quaint   _____   _____
7. dusk   _____   _____
8. fatigue   _____   _____
9. slender   _____   _____
10. imitate   _____   _____

Antonyms

✎ Exercise VT 2

Write two antonyms for each of the following words:

1. multiply   _____   _____
2. victory   _____   _____
3. rich   _____   _____
4. cheap   _____   _____
5. friend   _____   _____
6. expand   _____   _____
7. innocent   _____   _____
8. heaven   _____   _____
9. asleep   _____   _____
10. tame   _____   _____

REPRODUCIBLE

Vocabulary

Homophones, Homographs and Homonyms

✎ Exercise VT 3

Select the correct word from the brackets in these sentences:

1. The (boy/buoy) tied his dinghy to the harbour (boy/buoy).

2. A large (herd/heard) of animals was (herd/heard) moving through the jungle.

3. The (plane/plain) had to make a forced landing on the coastal (plane/plain).

4. Have you heard the (tail/tale) about the dog's (tail/tale)?

5. There was a (grate/great) fire burning in the (grate/great).

6. They (would/wood) do all they could to save the (would/wood) being cut.

7. That woman (road/rode) all day along the dusty (road/rode).

8. I don't know (weather/whether) to go out in the bad (weather/whether) today.

9. (They're/their) books are on the desk over (their/there).

10. I don't know if I can (bear/bare) to see my sister (bear/bare) in the shower.

REPRODUCIBLE

Vocabulary

Prefixes

✎ Exercise VT 4

Use prefixes to create antonyms of the following words:

1. healthy _____
2. truthful _____
3. attentive _____
4. experienced _____
5. respectful _____
6. satisfied _____
7. polite _____
8. visible _____
9. loyal _____
10. certain _____

✎ Exercise VT 5

Use prefixes to create new words of the following:

1. play _____
2. lead _____
3. septic _____
4. join _____
5. angle _____
6. ordinary _____
7. marine _____
8. sphere _____
9. gram _____
10. national _____

Suffixes

✎ Exercise VT 6

Use suffixes to create new words of the following:

1. disappoint _____
2. beauty _____
3. ugly _____
4. peace _____
5. water _____
6. notice _____
7. point _____
8. hero _____
9. print _____
10. patriot _____
11. apply _____
12. nominate _____
13. help _____
14. weak _____
15. able _____
16. child _____
17. taste _____
18. conclude _____
19. clarifiy _____
20. relate _____

REPRODUCIBLE

Vocabulary

Baby animals

✎ Exercise VT 7

What do you call the young of the following?

1. pigeon _____
2. fly _____
3. eagle _____
4. swan _____
5. human _____
6. horse _____
7. goat _____
8. cat _____
9. peacock _____
10. duck _____

Who lives there?

✎ Exercise VT 8

What do you call the homes of the following?

1. bear _____
2. wild rabbit _____
3. student _____
4. nun _____
5. soldier _____
6. monk _____
7. fox _____
8. Inuit _____
9. beaver _____
10. chicken _____

People's occupations

✎ Exercise VT 9

What do you call the occupations of the following?

1. A person who controls a business, a hotel, bank, etc _____
2. A person who interprets words spoken in a foreign language _____
3. A person who studies plants and trees _____
4. A person who writes plays or drama _____
5. A person who builds roads, railways, etc _____
6. A person who sends goods to foreign countries _____
7. A person who protects animals and birds hunted by man _____
8. A person in charge of prisoners _____
9. A person who tells the future from the stars _____
10. A person who writes books _____

REPRODUCIBLE

Vocabulary

Receptacles

✎ **Exercise VT 10**

What do you call the following containers or holders?

1. A small metal box for tea or coffee _____

2. A place where sacred relics are kept _____

3. A case for a dagger _____

4. A case that holds arrows _____

5. A vase for holding the ashes of the dead _____

6. A bag for carrying school books _____

7. A locked cupboard for holding possessions _____

8. A leather case for a pistol _____

9. A bottle for carrying drinks in one's pocket _____

10. A basket for carrying fish _____

Places

✎ **Exercise VT 11**

What do you call the following?

1. A building where corpses are burned _____

2. A place where ships are built _____

3. A building in which interesting and rare objects are displayed _____

4. A place for indoor or outdoor games with seats all around it _____

5. A place where whisky, gin or brandy is made _____

6. A building where grain is stored _____

7. A place where operations are performed _____

8. A home for orphans _____

9. A plot of land on which grapes are grown _____

10. A place where young trees and plants are grown _____

REPRODUCIBLE

Vocabulary

Forming nouns

✎ Exercise VT 12

Form nouns from the following words:

1. perfect _____
2. heavenly _____
3. empty _____
4. equal _____
5. dead _____
6. circular _____
7. chief _____
8. useless _____
9. valuable _____
10. young _____

Forming verbs

✎ Exercise VT 13

Form verbs from the following words:

1. authority _____
2. exception _____
3. acquittal _____
4. laughter _____
5. convenient _____
6. expectation _____
7. victim _____
8. wait _____
9. reflection _____
10. search _____

Forming adjectives

✎ Exercise VT 14

Form adjectives from the following words:

1. dotage _____
2. culmination _____
3. indicative _____
4. love _____
5. rejoice _____
6. speech _____
7. connection _____
8. suit _____
9. wait _____
10. anger _____

REPRODUCIBLE

Answers

Teachers Guide

Exercises to test yourself

Teachers Guide
Grammar

Nouns

 Exercise G 1

1. The reason I didn't go to **church** *(common)* on **Sunday** *(proper)* is that I was dining at **Mrs Graham's** *(proper)* **place** *(common)*.

2. Give **Stanley** *(proper)* my **love** *(abstract)* when you see him in **Sydney** *(proper)*.

3. After a good night's **sleep** *(common)*, my **neighbours** *(common)* **Stan** *(proper)* and **Shirley** *(proper)* caught a **limousine** *(common)* that took them to the **airport** *(common)*.

4. I had so much more **energy** *(abstract)* after eating a **meal** *(common)* of fine **food** *(common)*, including **meat** *(common)*, **vegetables** *(common)* and **cheeses** *(common)*.

5. **Carol** *(proper)* and I are going on **holiday** *(abstract)* to **Greece** *(proper)* in **September** *(proper)*

Proper nouns

 Exercise G 2:

1. The **doctor** *(common)* came on the last **Friday** *(proper)* in **April** *(proper)*.

2. The **author** *(common)* **F. Scott Fitzgerald** *(proper)* wrote a **novel** *(common)* titled **The Great Gatsby** *(proper)*.

3. Every **year** *(common)* many **people** *(common)* go to **London** *(proper)* in **England** *(proper)* to see **Buckingham Palace** *(proper)*, **Queen Elizabeth's** *(proper)* **home** *(common)*.

4. My **friend** *(common)* **Ashley** *(proper)* met **Sir Hubert Stanley** *(proper)* when she was in **Fiji** *(proper)*.

5. My **parents** *(common)*, **Mr and Mrs Reynolds** *(proper)*, live in **Australia** *(proper)* but I live in **Canada** *(proper)*.

Plurals

Exercise G 3

1. bluffs	11. criteria	21. diagnoses
2. leaves	12. energies	
3. salmon	13. synopses	
4. commanders-in-chief	14. minima	
5. archipelagos	15. ashes	
6. duties	16. princes	
7. minuses	17. errata	
8. mosquitoes	18. furniture	
9. dynamos	19. thieves	
10. antitheses	20. cliffs	

Pronouns

Exercise G 4

1. **We** *(personal)* left the room to search for **them** *(personal)*.

2. **She** *(personal)* asked **him** *(personal)* if **he** *(personal)* knew any of the people.

3. **It** *(personal)* isn't **your** *(possessive)* book, it's **mine** *(possessive)*!

4. **Whose** *(Interrogative)* book is **it** *(personal)*?

5. Are **these** *(demonstrative)* the animals that belong to **him** *(personal)*?

I and me

Exercise G 5

1. My dog and **I** are going for a walk.

2. When can Julie come with him and **me**?

3. She and **I** have decided not to go.

4. That is a secret between Lyn and **me**.

5. He put the books in front of **me**.

Prepositions

 Exercise G 6

1. The children climbed **into** bed **before** saying their prayers.

2. Gerry walked **across** the road to buy groceries **from** the store.

3. Jett jumped **over** the fence, ran **past** the house and **up** some stairs.

4. **Under** a tree lay a cat licking its fur.

5. **After** breakfast, Fred put on his boots and went for a run **in** the park.

Adjectives

 Exercise G 7

1. My **silly** (*descriptive*) sister behaved badly an annoyed **many** (*number/quantity*) people.

2. **That** (*demonstrative*) **sour-faced** (*descriptive*) woman wants dozens of **green** (*descriptive*) vegetables.

3. Does your friend have any of **those** (*demonstrative*) **exercise** (*descriptive*) books?

4. **Which** (*Interrogative*) of the **black** (*descriptive*) pens and **drawing** (*descriptive*) pages do you want?

5. When Toby hurt his **big** (*descriptive*) toe, he screamed for mum to help him.

Comparisons

 Exercise G 8

1. tall, taller, tallest
2. smart, smarter, smartest
3. good, better, best
4. thin, thinner, thinnest
5. little, less, least
6. many, more, most
7. much, more, most
8. pretty, prettier, prettiest
9. ugly, uglier, ugliest
10. grey, greyer, greyest

Verbs

 Exercise G 9

1. The small children **played** happily in the cubby-house.

2. The students **were given** their assignments.

3. The boys **will go** mountain-climbing next week.

4. Ricky **has had** a bad chest infection.

5. When she was ill, Emily **thought** she might die.

6. The horse **galloped** around the arena and then **jumped** the fence.

7. Iris **can do** the cooking tonight.

8. Did you **make** the bed this morning?

9. Children **enjoy** playing on computers.

10. Tigers **roam** jungles and are **hunted** by poachers.

Tenses

 Exercise G 10

1. Next week I **will stay** (or **will be staying**) in the hospital.

2. Right now I **demand** your attention!

3. Last night I **slept** at my aunt's place.

4. Our teacher **makes** us work hard.

5. Tom **polished** his shoes this morning.

6. Tomorrow night we **will eat** (or **we will be eating**) at the new restaurant.

7. She **swam** (or **was swimming**) up and down the pool's lanes.

8. Ted does not **approve** of killing animals.

9. The giggling of the girls **annoyed** the boys when they were in church.

10. As I **drove** (or **was driving**) along the road, a horse **appeared** in front of me.

Auxiliary verbs

 Exercise G 11

1. He **isn't** going.

2. I **was** asked to attend the concert.

3. Julia **is** doing her homework.

4. Alex **should** be handling this problem.

5. We **need** to see the doctor as soon as possible.

6. Oscar **will have** done his cleaning by noon.

7. Jessica **has** done the sweeping.

8. I **can** help you carry the luggage.

9. The officer **was** capturing the burglar.

10. The principal **will** help parents learn about their children.

Participles

 Exercise G 12

Identify the participles in the following sentences:

1. I have conquered my greatest fear: the fear of **flying**.

2. Daylight has **begun** and soon it will be time to leave.

3. As he patted the dog, Paul was **soothing** it.

4. Claire had **slept** restlessly all night.

5. We **watched** the children who were **sitting** around the fire.

6. The **wounded** and the **dying** were carried from the battle-field.

7. Having **finished** his meal, Chris went out.

8. I saw a star **shooting** across the sky last night.

9. We are **going** to Canberra by bus tomorrow.

10. Have you been **watching** the **boiling** eggs?

Gerunds

Exercise G 13

1. I don't like the sound of loud **shouting** next door.

2. What do you think about the sounds of **drumming** he's making?

3. The noisy **roaring** of the car engine upset the neighbours.

4. She heard the sound of **vacuuming** coming from her bedroom.

5. Alice received **falling** marks in English.

Adverbs

Exercise G 14

1. Life is difficult; **moreover**, you need to work **hard** in order to succeed.

2. When the train arrived **early**, hundreds of people pushed **forward** to get out of it **quickly**.

3. We were only able to get half of the groceries despite having **plenty** of money.

4. She felt, **however**, that the teacher was not as smart as she was.

5. He chatted to the girl in a **friendly** way and smiled **pleasantly** to strangers.

Passive voice

Exercise G 15

1. *Passive.* Granny cooked six meals.

2. *Active.* Jill was laughed at by Jack.

3. *Passive.* The gardener waters the plants every day.

4. *Passive.* Someone ordered a taxi to take the family home.

5. *Active.* The lawn was mown by Dad early this morning.

Sentences

Exercises G 16

1. After midnight my family and I drove to the city. – **Statment**

2. **D**o you enjoy playing tennis? – **Question**

3. Make a cake and do it now! – **Command**

4. **W**hat an amazing sight! – **Exaclamation**

5. **H**ow many people attended the concert? – **Question**

6. **T**here is a small bridge over the river. – **Statment**

7. **H**ow stupid of her to forget! – **Exclamation**

8. Hang on! – **Command**

9. It's dangerous to climb that tower. – **Statement**

10. **W**ith a choking cry, Jack fell to the ground. – **Statement**

Subject and object

Exercise G 17

1. **Davis** is the boy who scored the winning try.

2. **Gene and I** are going to the football match.

3. When are **you and Mum** heading for the beach?

4. **I** put the cat and dog into the car.

5. Every Christmas **Santa Claus** visits our house.

6. A frightening thing happened to **him and me**.

7. She ate **the baked dinner**.

8. Grandpa put **his socks** in the drawer.

9. Dogs chase **cats**.

10. Caspar was driving **the car** when it crashed.

Clauses

Exercise G 18

1. The water was icy **and the current was raging**.

2. Jean tried to run to safety **but the storm prevented her**.

3. **Unless he gets help,** it will be too late.

4. The car, **which carried two passengers**, drove into town.

5. I wanted to go to the concert **but my mother wouldn't let me**.

6. This is the book **that I own**.

7. I hoped to attend the market **which was held in the gardens**.

8. I wanted to play the piano **but she beat me to it**.

9. Unfortunately I can't play **because I've broken my finger**.

10. I used to know the boy **whom my classmates nicknamed Rusty**.

Phrases

Exercise G 19

1. The mother **of four children** leads a very busy life.

2. **With a big splash**, Jim fell into the lake.

3. **All of a sudden**, Jade fell off the slippery dip.

4. **After the question**s, the mayor replied **with much enthusiasm**.

5. **When we go out**, we usually head **for the city**.

6. All the people **in the room** began to stamp their feet **on the floor**.

7. The dog **with black and white spots** fetched the stick **for its master**.

8. When the baby cried **for its mother**, the nurse went **to its aid instead**.

9. **On his birthday**, Ricky had a cake **with chocolate icing and strawberry cream**.

10. The helicopter hovered **above the building** before landing **on the roof**.

Conjunctions

Exercise G 20

1. She went to the shops **where** she bought two new shirts.
2. Ann likes coffee **but** Vicki likes tea.
3. Mark got up late **as** it was Saturday.
4. The girl was laughing **and** crying.
5. Tony has a car **in which** he will go to town.
6. **Although** she felt ill she did not stop working.
7. He was angry **because** his father was late.
8. Emma went to bed **after** she cleaned her teeth.
9. He acted stupidly, **like** a monkey.
10. Will you stay here **while** I go somewhere?

Sentences: common problems

Exercise G 21

1. Swimming is one of the sports that **attracts** me.
2. A number of scholars **have** won admission to University.
3. A herd of animals **is** stampeding across the plains.
4. Salt and pepper **is** on the table.
5. The birds of summer **are** flying into our garden.
6. Everyone who **wants** to come **is** welcome.
7. He **smokes** every day – a silly habit!
8. Each of the boys **is** responsible for the silliness.
9. The flock of birds **has** taken off.
10. **Are** red, yellow and blue the colours you use to create secondary colours?

Paragraphs

Exercise G 22

Hi! It's me, the Easter Bunny!

Easter's just come and gone. Did you get your eggs a few days late? If you did, I'm truly sorry. It was not my fault. The fact is I was kidnapped and forced to spend the whole holiday period inside a bedroom cupboard. My kidnapper, Jonathon Livermore, (known as J.L.), tried to deliver the eggs. But he messed up the whole thing.

You're probably asking what sort of a person would kidnap the Easter Bunny? The thing is J.L's not really such a bad kid. He was trying to make friends. But he went about it the wrong way and mucked things up.

I first met J.L. behind my chocolate factory. Dressed in a cowboy suit, he was playing by himself, trying to lasso a fence post. I was stacking crates of last-minute Easter egg orders when he saw me.

"Hey!" he yelled. "Come over here!"

I took one look at him and turned away. I had no time for loud-mouthed little boys.

"Come and play with me!" he demanded.

I took no notice.

He strode up. "Play with me!"

"I'm busy", I said. "Go find a human your own age to play with."

Punctuation

Capital letters

 ### Exercise P 1

1. **U**nder the **B**oardwalk is a song by **T**he **R**olling **S**tones.

2. **R**obbery **U**nder **A**rms was written by a famous novelist.

3. **H**ave you read **C**onfessions of a **L**iar and **T**hief?

4. **I L**ove a **S**unburnt **C**ountry is a poem by the **A**ustralian, **D**orothea **M**ackellar.

5. **T**he choir sang the national anthem, "**A**dvance **A**ustralia **F**air".

6. **W**hile on holiday in **N**ew **Y**ork, **A**merica, **S**andy and **I** went to the top of the **E**mpire **S**tate **B**uilding.

7. **M**y friend, who **I** meet the first **T**uesday of every month, is **P**rincess **M**arcia **J**ames.

8. **W**hile visiting **H**enry last **O**ctober, **I** was lucky enough to meet his grandmother who lives on **R**andwick **R**oad.

9. **E**very summer my family goes on holidays to **W**ollongong **NSW**.

10. **T**he **C**ountess of **Y**ork presented me with a trophy. **L**ater, the countess and **I** had dinner together.

Full stops

 ### Exercise P 2

She had hiked for hours. Her head ached and she was thirsty. When she reached the next road, she decided to take the left fork. She felt pleased with her decision when she arrived at the motel. It had been a long trek.

Commas

 ### Exercise P 3

1. Peter teases his sister, annoys his parents and frightens the neighbours.

2. She stopped, regained her breath, looked behind her and then went on running.

3. The monster had crossed eyes, a warted nose, purple cheeks, a crazy haircut and fifteen fingers on each hand.

4. The huge beast, as big as an elephant, lumbered through the jungle.

5. With a splash, the stick hit the water and the dog dived in for it.

Semicolons

 Exercise P 4

1. Penny tried to ride the horse; it wasn't easy as she was inexperienced.

2. The first step to cooking on a barbeque; put on your apron.

3. At the concert we saw a band playing rock and roll; an acrobat who was amazing; a singer with a husky voice; and a magician whose act went terribly wrong.

4. The girl was like her sister; long-legged, blonde and very shy.

5. He always took short cuts; as a result he often became lost.

Colons

 Exercise P 5

1. You have only one person to blame: yourself.

2. There are two rules: you must keep your room clean and pick up your belongings.

3. There's one thing my brother's good at: getting into trouble.

4. If you want to find out: go to the shed and check out the shelves.

5. Here is what I think: you only get one life, so take good care of it.

Quotation Marks

 Exercise P 6

1. "I have won", said Linda, "a trip for two to America. We'll be going next week."

2. Trinity said, "I can't believe it's true! Are you kidding me?"

3. "Would I tell a lie?" Linda replied. "Of course it's true."

4. "You lucky thing!" her sister said. "I wish I could come."

5. "Well, you can't", said Trinity. "It's only for mum and me."

Brackets

 Exercise P 7

1. Chris, Bill and Pat (Pat is a home-maker) are all coming to dinner.

2. At the party were Elysse, Andrew (the boy I told you about) and Marg.

3. After the drive, we returned the car (a Holden ute) to the garage.

4. Barry spent fifteen minutes (far too long) trying on a pair of boots.

5. During the tour they visited numerous cities (but why not, I wondered, Paris and London?) in just ten days.

Dashes

 Exercise P 8

1. His sister skipped school – so she said.

2. My mother's car – the one she drives every day – needs repairs.

3. They tell me he is an angry kind of man – I don't know him.

4. Sandwiches, pies, tarts – all of these were for lunch.

5. Who do you want to speak to – Jerry or Terry?

Hyphens

 Exercise P 9

1. Carl is green-eyed, big-nosed and bird-brained.

2. When I did the problem, my answer was twenty-five and three-quarters.

3. Dad is a do-it-yourself handyman who is over-eager to please Mum.

4. The man-eating lion performed tricks in the circus in front of wide-eyed children.

5. He was an ex-army officer who has retired because he is a semi-invalid.

Ellipses

Exercise P 10

1. Well, I was going, but then...

2. What the ... is he doing with that knife?

3. Mark crashed to the floor ... only much later did he come to.

4. The problem was, would the lawyer go to court, or ...

5. I bought two cakes for ten dollars ... at that price I could have made five myself.

Apostrophes

Exercise P 11

1. After the run we put the dogs' coats on them and then we went to Mark's place.

2. That's the girl I told you about, the one who doesn't go to school.

3. We can't come to Angus' party next week because we're going on holidays.

4. It's impossible to tell whether or not it's alive.

5. That is James' dog and Susie's cat.

6. The dog sat and scratched its back leg.

7. The man stole the ladies' handbags.

8. She went to get the men's hats and the boys' scarves.

9. I'm going to have to get the cat's dinner ready.

10. We're afraid she's going to be too late for the show's opening.

Punctuation in poetry

Exercise P 12

Who has seen the wind?
Neither I nor you:
but when the leaves are trembling,
The wind is passing through.

Who has seen the wind?
Neither you nor I
But when the trees bow down their heads,
The wind is passing by.

Christina Rossetti

Word Usage

Affect and effect

Exercise W 1

1. To **affect** a change, we must employ a new teacher.

2. The **effect** of the hail was to damage our home.

3. The strike **affected** the way we travelled into town.

4. We felt the **effect** of cuts to our water supply.

5. What was the **effect** of possums in your roof?

Among and between

Exercise W 2

1. Mum divided the cakes **among** Shelley, Mikki and Aaron.

2. I can't decide from **among** the hundreds of choices.

3. I have to choose **between** Jack and Rick for my team.

4. We walked **among** the many trees in the forest.

5. I live my life **between** my mum's house and my dad's house.

Articles A, an and the

Exercise W 3

1. Bill went for **a** walk up a long track. **The** track led to a mountain.

2. Penny owns **a** dog, **an** owl and **the** cat you saw yesterday.

3. Pass me **a** pear, please. Yes, **the** green one will do.

4. Pam has **a** small doll. **The** doll went missing yesterday.

5. It is **an** honour to serve you.

Bought and brought

Exercise W 4

1. We spent two dollars and **bought** a loaf of bread.

2. What have you **brought** to sell at the market?

3. Max and Ann have **brought** along their old clothes.

4. He **bought** a fast, roomy, new car.

5. I was surprised when he **brought** along a dinosaur bone for the display.

Bring and take

Exercise W 5

1. I shall **take** my cat when I go on holidays.

2. **Bring** your cat to me.

3. I must (**bring** or **take**) my medicine with me.

4. Shall I **take** her some cake?

5. When are you going to (**bring** or **take**) your project to school?

Can and may

 Exercise W 6

1. **Can** you help me with these equations?

2. **May** I go to the toilet?

3. **May** Jill and I take the last cakes?

4. **Can** you direct me to the highway?

5. **May** I spend fifty dollars at the shops, Mum?

Double negatives

 Exercise W 7

1. I didn't do **anything**.

2. I don't **ever** go to the movies.

3. Can you **ever** do anything right?

4. I was going.

5. Give me that or I will never give you **anything**.

Either and or

 Exercise W 8

1. I'm going to **choose** either these tools or those.

2. Either you or Emily **is** coming with me.

3. Either the man or the women **are** catching the bus.

4. Which do you prefer: either the boys or the girl to **act** as our mascot?

5. Either Mum or Dad **wants** to know the answer.

Good and well

 ## Exercise W 9

1. Did he do **well** when he was competing?

2. We found that it was a **good** piece of pie.

3. She did **well** to please her mother.

4. Heath writes **well**.

5. She is **well**-mannered.

Less and fewer

 ## Exercise W 10

1. There is **less** sugar in this bag than that.

2. In our country there are **fewer** sheep than in your country.

3. Our teacher gave us **less** homework than yesterday.

4. Because of good signage, there are **fewer** deaths on the roads.

5. As I'm on a diet, I now eat **less** fat than I ate before.

Lend and loan

 ## Exercise W 11

1. Do you think he'll **lend** me his book?

2. Ray gave me a **loan** of his book.

3. When we get to school, I'll ask to have a **loan** of the homework answers.

4. Give me a **loan** of that case or I'll report you.

5. I'm going to **lend** him my favourite computer game.

Lie and lay

 Exercise W 12

1. When he finished **laying** down the books, he picked up his pen.

2. Is he **lying** or is he telling the truth?

3. Because I was tired, I **lay** down.

4. All afternoon Granny has **lain** on the lounge.

5. Pop has already **laid** dishes on the dinner table.

Neither and nor

 Exercise W 13

1. This tool suits neither the **needs** of the mechanic nor his offsider.

2. Neither Tom nor his sisters **are** in the house.

3. I **want** neither the apples nor the banana.

4. Neither the boys nor their sister **is** playing indoors.

5. Instead of the cake, they **prefer** sandwiches.

Past and passed

 Exercise W 14

Use the correct word in the brackets in the following sentences:

1. We strolled **past** the derelict houses.

2. He **passed** the ball from his friend to his teacher.

3. The runner was first **past** the line.

4. He is well **past** the age of retirement.

5. Under the bridge he dawdled, over the hill and **past** the barn.

Shall and will

Exercise W 15

1. I **shall** try even harder to get first place in class.

2. We **will** arrive at your place this afternoon.

3. She **will** catch the bus tomorrow morning.

4. I **will** bake a cake for the fete, just you wait and see.

5. The girl covered her ears and said, "I **will** not do it!"

They're, there and their

Exercise W 16

1. Do you know if **they're** going to the show?

2. The children put **their** toys away after playing.

3. Sally and Todd arranged for **their** car to be cleaned.

4. Don't put it **there**!

5. Sit with that woman over **there**.

6. John and Volda have sold **their** house.

7. We don't know if **they're** arriving today.

8. After breakfast Aaron and Mikayla put on **their** school clothes.

9. The ducks were waddling over **there** to the pond.

10. I swept the yard and then I had to pick up **their** toys.

Two, to, too

Exercise W 17

1. We are going to Wollongong, **too.**

2. I thought I would take the **two** dogs.

3. It is **too** cold **to** go outside without a warm coat.

4. She will come with us **too**, so be prepared.

5. After we go **to** Melbourne, we'll travel with James, **too**.

6. Would you allow me to come with you, **too**?

7. We have **two** cats and three dogs.

8. The explorers walked **to** the North Pole.

9. We're going up the mountain and from there down **to** the river.

10. I hope you don't expect me to work **too**.

Who and whom?

 Exercise W 18

1. They asked to **whom** I was speaking.

2. Is that the boy with **whom** you went to camp?

3. **Who** is he taking on his date?

4. Mum knows the lady **wh**o wins all the prizes.

5. He is the person **whom** I wanted to see.

What and which

 Exercise W 19

1. **Which** person invented the submachine gun?

2. Do you know **which** of the three children missed school today?

3. **Which** elephant is the one that has tusks?

4. I'm not sure **what** dress to choose out of all these in the shop.

5. **What** was the name of the tribe that conquered the village?

Which and that

 Exercise W 20

1. Where is the suit **that** you've decided to wear?

2. His ponies, **which** he kept in the paddock, are now missing.

3. Paul has a green car **that** he drives to university.

4. His cooking, **which** we used to enjoy every night, has not been as tasty as usual.

5. It is exactly the sort of dress **that** I always choose to wear.

When and where

 Exercise W 21

1. Illiteracy is the condition of a person who is unable to read or write.

2. Erosion occurs where wind wears the rock away.

3. A stalactite occurs where a rock is formed by constant water dripping on it.

4. Pollution occurs where the environment is spoiled by man-made waste.

5. Puberty is the time when a person is first able to produce offspring.

Alliteration

 Exercise W 22

1. Frogs frolic fancy-free forever

2. Grandmothers get grey-haired and gorgeous with age.

3. Cars creep across the crowded car park.

4. Whispering winds whip up water.

5. Dancers delight dozens of day-trippers.

6. Balls – bright and bouncy – bump bystanders.

7. Swiftly swallows swoop and soar.

8. Dazzling days delight dreamers.

9. Enormous elephants engage our attention.

10. Dreary days drift and don't delay.

Ambiguity

 Exercise W 23

1. I promise I'll give you a diamond ring tomorrow.

2. A farmer found a cow by a stream.

3. Flying planes can be a dangerous occupation.

4. Both my mother and I are glad I'm a man.

5. They are dogs used for hunting.

Clichés

 Exercise W 24

1. The teacher scolded me so much I decided to do my homework the next time.

2. Getting into trouble made me feel as though I was full of steam.

3. My sister knows exactly how to aggravate me.

4. I was in class so long that I lost focus and no longer listened.

5. Don't get so upset.

6. She likes to brag about her accomplishments.

7. That was so easy a child could have done it.

8. That was difficult to accept.

9. He was taking whatever opportunity he could.

10. She was making up the story as she spoke.

Overworked words

 ## Exercise W 25

1. The meat pies were **delicious**.

2. She **won** a prize in the competition.

3. The skaters gave a **graceful** display on the ice.

4. The rotten prawns had a **putrid** smell.

5. We had to sit through a **tedious** performance.

6. I **caught** a bad cold after someone sneezed on me.

7. There was a **colourful** display of flowers in the show.

8. I had a **painful** experience at the doctor's.

9. He is a **dangerous** driver.

10. She had a **dislocated** knee after the hockey game.

Metaphors

 ## Exercise W 26

1. Time **is a thief.**

2. Life **is a struggle.**

3. Death **is a permanent sleep.**

4. Choices **are crossroads.**

5. My mother **is a rock.**

6. The moon **is a white face in heaven.**

7. The glutton **is a pig.**

8. The road **was a never-ending ribbon of tar.**

9. The house **was a garbage tip.**

10. My school **is a prison.**

Similes

 Exercise W 27

1. Her eyes were as blue **as the deep sea.**

2. He runs **like a frightened gazell**

3. He fights as though **his life depends on victory.**

4. My father's car races **as if it was powered by a jet engine.**

5. She was shaking **like a leaf in the wind.**

6. Mark was driving **as though he was possessed.**

7. She walks as gracefully **as a prima donna ballerina.**

8. He was brave as a **lion in a struggle for life and death.**

9. The rain falls **like shattered pieces of glass.**

10. Exams are **as difficult as climbing Mount Everest.**

Personification

 Exercise W 28

1. The thunder **grumbled as though its belly ached**.

2. The flowers **waltzed** in the gentle breeze.

3. The words **appeared to leap off the paper** as she read the story.

4. The phone **awakened** with a mighty ring

5. The fire **ran wild**.

6. The birds **danced** in the morning sun.

7. The time **flew by** as the children played.

8. The bees **played hide and seek with the flowers** as they buzzed from one to another.

9. The wind **howled its mighty objection**.

10. The snow **swaddled the earth like a mother would her infant child.**

Vocabulary

Synonyms

 Exercise V 1

1. start, commence, open
2. deceive, swindle, trick
3. risky, hazardous, unsafe
4. dreary, gloomy, cheerless
5. achieve, gain, acquire
6. glory, respect, praise
7. uneducated, stupid, untaught
8. error, flaw, defect
9. pastime, sport, fun, recreation
10. fear, dread, fright

Antonyms

 Exercise V 2

1. reject
2. natural
3. disperse
4. forbid
5. poison
6. never
7. descend
8. pleased
9. robust
10. giant

Homophones

 ## Exercise V 3

1. I was wearing my **new** blue jeans which I'm sure you **knew**.

2. He didn't know **where** they were going and so didn't know what to **wear**.

3. **Two** of the students are going **to** the park **too**.

4. Dad told me to come over **here** and then said, "Can't you **hear** me?"

5. I think the answer to your question is **no**, but I really don't **know**.

6. **Would** you prefer to live near a **wood** or a town?

7. As I wasn't taught the **right** way, I'm afraid I don't **write** very neatly.

8. **Which** spell did the nasty **witch** use?

9. I didn't listen to the **weather** report so I don't know **whether** or not to wear a raincoat.

10. When the teacher walked **past** we **passed** out homework notes.

Onomatopoeia

 ## Exercise V 4

1. The microwave oven **beeped** when the food was cooked.

2. I heard the **clattering** of the horse's hoofs as it approached.

3. The **drip, drip, drip** of that tap is driving me crazy.

4. My teacher **mumbles** so much I can't understand what he's saying.

5. Sausages were **sizzling** in the frypan.

6. When the wind rose, it **rattled** windows and doors.

7. The children went **whizzing** around on the merry-go-round.

8. When he pulled the keys out of his pocket, they **jangled**.

9. **Knock, knock**! Who's there?

10. the cork was pulled from the bottle with a loud **pop**.

Suffixes

✏ Exercise V 5

1. weather-wise
2. kindness
3. humanoid
4. flexibility
5. digestive
6. hopeless
7. equalise
8. friendship
9. meeting
10. dusty

Prefixes

✏ Exercise V 6

1. infrared
2. multitasking
3. kilograms
4. self-help
5. afternoon
6. ultra-transparent
7. tricycle (bicycle)
8. triangle
9. cyberspace
10. counteract

Animals

✏ Exercises V 7

1. cygnets
2. leverets
3. ducklings
4. parr
5. babies, infants, children
6. nymph
7. grub
8. eaglet
9. squab
10. peachick

Homes of creatures

✏ Exercise V 8

1. shell
2. web
3. dove-cot
4. nest
5. shell
6. coup
7. form
8. fortress
9. hive
10. stable

People's occupations

 Exercise V 9

1. cabinet-maker
2. artist, illustrator
3. architect
4. astronomer
5. entomologist
6. etymologist
7. draughtsperson
8. playwright
9. editor
10. exporter

Receptacles

 Exercise V 10

1. brief-case
2. cauldron
3. urn
4. chest
5. locker
6. portfolio
7. quiver
8. suitcase
9. petrol-tank
10. flask

Places

 Exercise V 11

1. kitchen
2. airfield, aerodrome
3. cemetery, crypt
4. emporium
5. reservoir
6. church
7. harbour
8. alley
9. orchard
10. shipyard

Collective nouns

Exercise V 12

1. school, shoal
2. band, pack
3. flock, flight
4. group, choir
5. swarm
6. troupe
7. flock
8. litter
9. crowd, throng, multitude
10. crew
11. host
12. kindle
13. posse, patrol
14. mob
15. staff
16. troupe
17. tuft, head
18. suite
19. galaxy
20. bouquet, bunch, arrangement

Forming nouns

Exercise V 13

1. favouritism
2. freedom
3. creation
4. argument
5. encouragement
6. obedience
7. responsibility
8. mockery
9. bluntness
10. extremity

Forming adjectives

Exercise V 14

1. learner
2. satisfactory
3. noticeable
4. saleable
5. popular
6. spiritual
7. original
8. visionary
9. central
10. foggy

Forming verbs

 Exercise V 15

1. poverty
2. admittance
3. choice
4. explorer (or exploration)
5. concealment
6. growth
7. fluency
8. purity
9. cloudiness (or cloud)
10. truth

Exercises to Test Yourself
Grammar

Nouns

 Exercise GT 1

1. petunias (common noun)
2. love (abstract noun)
3. Samuel (proper noun)
4. litter (collective noun and common noun)
5. energy (abstract noun)
6. hatred (abstract noun)
7. avenue (proper noun and common noun)
8. Jones (proper noun)
9. mass (abstract noun)
10. flock (collective noun)

Singular

 Exercise GT 2

1. crisis
2. ellipsis
3. singular
4. sheep
5. knife
6. beau
7. person
8. citizen
9. trauma
10. stimulus

Plurals

 Exercise GT 3

1. parentheses
2. radii
3. logos
4. messieurs
5. baggage
6. mothers-in-law
7. staffs
8. witches
9. glories
10. dynamos
11. echoes
12. chassis
13. nuclei
14. shelves

Pronouns

 Exercise GT 4

Suggested Answers

1. **You** and **I** are going to take **him** to the movies.
2. My three year old dressed **himself** this morning.
3. This is the book **that** everyone has been recommending recently,
4. **Who** were you talking to on the phone?
5. I need **this** signed right away.
6. **Anyone** can draw, though **some** are better than **others**.

Prepositions

 Exercise GT 5

1. We offered our **congratulations** to the couple **on** getting engaged.
2. Wesley was **accompanied by** his best friend.
3. Dad was **pleased with** my high scores in the test.
4. I don't like people who **profit by** over-taxing customers.
5. My brother is pleased to be **independent from** our parents.
6. The land lies **adjacent to** the house.

7. When you were small, did you **succeed at** school?

8. Mabel is always **boasting about** her garden display.

9. The lawn was **covered with** leaves.

Adjectives

 Exercise GT 6

1. **twenty (number/quantity), cricket (descriptive)**

2. **terrible (descriptive), their (possessive)**

3. **which (interrogative), wiggly (descriptive), sad (descriptive)**.

4. **that (demonstrative), silly (descriptive), many (number/quantity)**

5. **famous (descriptive), delicious (descriptive), pumpkin (descriptive)**

Making Comparisons

 Exercise GT 7

1. **wiser, wisest**

2. **more frugal, most frugal**

3. **merrier, merriest**

4. **shorter, shortest**

5. **more beautiful, most beautiful**

6. **angrier, angriest**

7. **more colourful, most colourful**

8. **more popular, most popular**

9. **steeper, steepest**

10. more pleasant, most pleasant

Verbs

 Exercise GT 8

1. burglar (sneaks, creeps, steals)

2. drunk (staggers, meanders, mutters)

3. old person (shuffles, hobbles, forgets)

4. mice (scamper, skitter, squeak)

5. skater (glides, pirouettes, slides)

6. waves (undulate, wash, break)

7. flowers (droop, wilt, grow)

8. dog (prances, chases, bounds)

9. soldier (marches, trudges, fights)

10. queen (reigns, leads, waves)

Tenses

 Exercise GT 9

1. present tense
2. present tense
3. future tense
4. present tense
5. past tense
6. past tense
7. past tense
8. present tense
9. past tense
10. past tense

Auxiliary Verbs

 Exercise GT 10

may, might, must, be, being, been, is, was, were, do, does, did, have, had, has, should, could, would, will, can, shall, am, are, ought, dare

Participles

 Exercise GT 11

1. The man is **approaching** the station where a train is **waiting**.
2. **Running** around the oval are thirteen **panting** athletes.
3. The presenter has **talked** for three **boring** hours.
4. We have had **enough** of his endless speech.
5. Joel is a comedian, **playing** to an audience too afraid to laugh.
6. **Lying** on the grass, Anthony and Kelly saw a **shooting** star.
7. Visibly **shaken**, the woman walked away from the wrecked car.
8. I could tell someone was home because the chimney was **smoking**.

Gerunds

Exercise GT 12

1. **Sneezing** all morning exhausted me.
2. Paul hates **cooking** because he's hopeless at it.
3. At the wedding, he finally gave **dancing** a chance.
4. My favourite activity on a Saturday morning is **reading** the paper.
5. **Doing** chores all day is never a fun way to spend the weekend.

Adverbs

Exercise GT 13

1. He has **almost** managed to perform **weekly** for two months **now**.
2. He put the bags **outside under** the apple tree.
3. Every day I swim **fast** to warm myself up in the cold pool.
4. **Never** have I seen anyone walk like that!
5. My grandfather is **too** old to walk **anywhere** now.
6. The pie I made **yesterday** was **surprisingly** good.
7. I drove **across** the country to deliver the car to the new owner.
8. The Christmas tree was **very** tall, and illuminated **brilliantly**.
9. She is **almost always** cheerful.
10. I wanted a higher score on the exam, but I didn't work hard **enough**.

Sentences

Exercise GT 14

1. You should check your weight after eating all that fatty food. (statement)
2. What an amazing person you are! (exclamation)
3. What are you doing with that handgun? (question)
4. Neither the cow nor the horse was found. (statement)
5. Were you part of the crowd that attended the rock concert? (question)
6. How many times have I told you not to do that? (question)
7. Wow, I didn't know you could do that! (exclamation)
8. Milly has three sisters – Tilly, Jilly and Petunia. (statement)
9. Do it right now! (command)
10. I suppose you'll never forgive me; is that right? (question)

Subject

 Exercise GT 15

1. **A large car** stopped in front of our house.

2. **His constant drumming** annoyed the neighbours.

3. **Whom to hire** is a difficult question.

4. "**I love you**", is what the man said to his fiancé.

5. It was **a** gift from him to them.

6. **Green** is my favourite colour.

7. **A Christmas card** from Aunt Judy arrived in the mail.

8. **The plumber** fixed the pipes under the sink.

Object

 Exercise GT 16

1. Give the football to **me**, not him.

2. In the jungle, lions hunt for **prey**.

3. After the final song, the drummer hurled **his sticks** at the crowd.

4. Marcus stunned the **giraffe** with a radar gun.

5. Heaping **his plate** with fried chicken, Dad winked at the cook.

6. Mike ran past **the group of people** who were jogging.

7. Grandad gave me **the cricket bat** he used as a kid.

8. Rachel won a **prize** at the science fair.

Phrases

 ### Exercise GT 17

1. He slipped the envelope **under the door** and then left **to catch a bus.**

2. Putting the slipper **on his left foot**, he hobbled **out of the room**.

3. She's a singer **with a wide repertoire** who always pleases her audiences.

4. **On the patchwork mat** sits a fat, white cat.

5. Can you please put string **around the parcel** and then tie the knot?

6. Our class obtained the first three places **in the spelling bee**.

7. Do you know the song **from beginning to end**?

8. She helps me **in so many ways.**

9. Don't put it **over there**!

10. **Over the moon** jumped the cow, followed by the dog.

Clauses

 ### Exercise GT 18

1. **You'll be much happier** when the trouble passes.

2. **Whenever lazy students whine**, my teacher laughs.

3. Tony ran for the paper towels **as cola spilled over the table.**

4. **Because my dog loves pizza crusts**, he never barks at the deliveryman.

5. A person **who eats too many sugary foods** will soon develop rotten teeth.

6. You really do not want to know **what Aunt Nancy adds to her stew.**

7. Bill blushed **because Di smiled at him**.

8. We all cheered **when the football team scored a goal.**

9. I don't like **people who lie and cheat.**

10. My sister isn't very popular **because she gossips too much.**

Conjunctions

 ## Exercise GT 19

1. We stayed indoors **because** it was raining.

2. I'm wearing a woolly jumper **although** the temperature is in the high thirties.

3. We shopped at the supermarket **then** went home.

4. He ran **and** jumped **and** whooped with joy.

5. I was feeling tired **so** I went home.

6. We looked after Mimi's dog **while** Mimi was overseas.

7. Bob was tired **and** hungry so he cooked dinner and went to bed.

8. Jack went to bed **as** did Judy. (or Jack and Judy went to bed.)

9. He washed the dishes **before** I dried them.

10. Rick started up the car's engine **while** Jack listened for the noise.

Voice

 ## Exercise GT 20

1. (passive) The civilian arrested the man.

2. (active) The revolver was lifted by Maud and the trespasser was shot.

3. (active) Evidence of ice have been found on Mars by scientists.

4. (active) Diamonds are being stolen from the shop by thieves.

5. (passive) The postman delivered a letter to Mr Jones.

6. (active) The report will be presented by the group next week.

7. (active) Many difficult questions were asked by the teacher.

8. (passive) Some bullies stole my bike and helmet.

9. (active) The book is being read by most of the class.

10. (passive) The stove was accidentally left on by me when I left the house.

PUNCTUATION

Capital letters

Exercise PT 1

1. When we went to Canberra we drove over Lake Burley Griffin and visited the National War Museum.

2. Do you know that my father is Sir William Condon?

3. Susie and I live in Mount Street but next May we are moving to Broadway Lane.

4. Last Tuesday I visited Dr Marshall for a check-up.

5. Her Majesty Queen Elizabeth II lives in Buckingham Palace in London.

Full stops and commas

Exercise PT 2

1. I swept the yard, weeded the garden, and then I had to cook dinner for Jim, Danny and John.

2. He bought a fast, green car.

3. My brother Larry, who is usually a healthy man, now has a fever.

4. It is a great honour to introduce my friends, Ann and Julie.

5. He asked question after question and then he paused, saying, "I think you have the flu."

6. Mum always puts fruit into my lunchbox. My favourites are apples, bannanas and pears.

7. The man playing blackjack was dealt a three, a two and a queen.

Brackets and dashes

 Exercise PT 3

1. The Second World War (1939-1945) involved many nations, including England and Germany.

2. It was a tough match to win – Victorian players are rough.

3. Vicki wore a dress (a prized possession) to the ball.

4. The woman was lying on the bed – dead.

5. She assembled all the ingredients – flour, margarine, eggs, sugar and sultanas – and started making the cake.

6. Cheval place (in Chester) is where you'll find the Princess Theatre.

Hyphens

 Exercise PT 4

1. Jerry is so self-reliant, he works non-stop from morning to night in the multi-storeyed office block.

2. While out walking, I collected grass-seeds in my hiking boots.

3. As I made too many errors, I re-signed the letter to impress my difficult-to-please boss.

4. Mum says my sister's boyfriend is a good-for-nothing who ought to get himself a decent job.

5. We bought home-made marmalade from a middle-aged woman at the fete.

Colons and semi-colons

 Exercise PT 5

1. This year I am studying these subjects: English, biology, art and history.

2. Jack strolled along the beach picking up shells; then he found a prize piece of driftwood.

3. Jim locked himself in his room; his team had lost the cricket match.

4. My mother taught me two golden rules: I was to do my best and always tell the truth.

5. The rocket rose; it twisted in the air; it suddenly burst into flames.

Apostrophes

 Exercise PT 6

1. It's time we were all in bed, seeing as she's asked us five times already.

2. Julia and Matty's house is built next to Rob's.

3. Can you collect its blanket and give it to the neighbour's son Alex?

4. I couldn't have cared less about homework, but my two friends' efforts made me change my mind.

5. Jagger's and McCartney's songwriting skills were distinct and different.

Ellipses

 Exercise PT 7

1. What the ... is going on?

2. I put it somewhere ... now where was it?

3. I was going to, but I forget ... what it was I was going to do.

4. Look there ... can you see it?

5. It's a monstrous ...

Quotation marks

 Exercise PT 8

"I'm pregnant", said Mum.

I stared at her. I couldn't believe what she had said. "You're what?"

Mum picked up her cup of tea. She took a sip. "I'm going to have a baby."

Was I hearing right?

"You can't have a baby!" I said.

Mum and Dad smiled at one another, like I'd said something really funny.

"Oh, and why not?" said Mum.

"You're too old."

"I'm only thirty two. Not too old."

"But ..." I didn't know what else to say.

Punctuation

 ## Exercise PT 9

"He's too skinny." The stout Indian with the long, black moustache looked at Amin, the four year old boy in front of him.

"But he's strong for his age", said Amin's father, Sa'id. "If you give him good food as you promised, he will surely fatten up."

Amin's stomach ached. But he wasn't worried about that. His stomach often ached from lack of food. What most ached at that moment was his heart. All through the night just past he had listened to his parents talking. His mother had cried again and again. She and his father talked about him, their second-youngest son. Papa talked about indenturing him to the Indian. Amin didn't understand the word "indentured" but he knew that his father wanted to sell him to the Indian.

Once before now the Indian had come to his village. He had bought four children, including Amin's older sister Zarina and his brother Suleiman.

"Four hundred rupees", the Indian said. "That's all your skinny son is worth."

"Four hundred rupees will only feed my family for one week", said Sa'id. "Please, kind sir, could you make his price one thousand rupees?"

The Indian laughed, loud and long. To Amin he sounded like a hyena. "Surely you jest?"

"Nine hundred?"

"I will give you five hundred."

The haggling went on and on.

WORD USAGE

✏ Exercise WT 1

1. Share the sweets **among** the five children, please.

2. **May** I borrow your lawn-mower?

3. There are **fewer** people here than I thought there might be.

4. Shane is the boy **whom** we were discussing last night.

5. Penny owns **the** dog you can see over there.

6. Matthew found **an** orange-coloured cat in the lane.

7. Have you **brought** some food along today to share with us all?

8. He has **less** to worry about than you have.

9. Are you going to **lie** down and have a nap?

10. Please don't **bring** that old thing to the party tomorrow.

✏ Exercise WT 2

1. She is the person **who** forgot her permission note.

2. I don't know her very **well**.

3. **Lay** that book on the desk, please.

4. Hal had **laid** his belongings on the bed.

5. He **lied** about where he was that day.

6. When I go to camp, what should I **take**?

7. I can't see **who** is over there.

8. Please **lend** me your favourite book.

9. I **shall** depart by train in the morning.

10. They **will** go or there will be trouble.

Exercise WT 3

1. The rules take **effect** straight away.

2. How did it **affect** you having a stranger in your home?

3. **Take** that mess away from here!

4. **Can** you fix the broken pipe?

5. Sir, **may** I go to the toilet, please?

6. Neither Rob nor **I** have been to the opera.

7. She did **well** in the yearly exams.

8. Her drawings, **which** were excellent, were chosen for the display.

9. Give me the clothes **that** need ironing.

10. Emily has a new baby **who** is named Noah.

 Exercise WT 4

1. **What** book are you going to read next?

2. **Their** stories didn't tally, so I knew they were **lying**.

3. Put the machine over **there** and leave it to me to fix it.

4. The detective examined **their** clothes for evidence.

5. Will you please **lend** me your two books?

6. Are you going **to** the cinema with those **two**?

7. She is **too** dishonest for me to trust her.

8. He hasn't **anything** to say about the accident.

9. Matty **can** hardly wait until his birthday.

10. We all **swam** at the beach yesterday.

Exercise WT 5

1. The crowd **was** a huge one – over three thousand people.

2. The crowd of three thousand **is** behaving badly.

3. Three thousand people **are** behaving badly.

4. Since the committee is in charge, **it** has the final decision.

5. Neither the dogs nor the cat **was** found to have the disease.

6. A pair of scissors **was** used.

7. In the news **are** many stories about car accidents.

8. Fifty head of cattle **is** being sold tomorrow at the auction.

9. Thanks were given to the woman who **had** organised the event.

10. This kind of apple **is** delicious.

 ## Exercise WT 6

1. The **youngest** of the three girls is called Sally.

2. These kinds of mistakes **are** very costly.

3. Of the four children, the **eldest** is the most educated.

4. This year there were **fewer** prizes.

5. Every cow and bull **was** sold.

6. The fastest in the world, the aeroplane **is** now being mass produced.

7. My dog was the **most** valuable in the show.

8. Jimmy is the **tallest** boy in the class.

9. If he and **I** ever meet, we're sure to like one another.

10. **Who** did you see at the movies?

Exercise WT 7

1. I am not sure if either of the two girls **is** to come with us.

2. Neither the men nor the woman **is** sitting on the jury.

3. I wish that my neighbour would stop playing that **continuous** music.

4. I don't care about music one way or another; I'm really **disinterested**.

5. Robin was **uninterested** in her mother's new dress.

6. The train was **stationary**, waiting for passengers.

7. I must **have** lost my necklace when I was at your place.

8. We walked **around** the property looking for the missing horses.

9. The boy I saw must have been **about** seven years old.

10. Lucy took out her **stationery** and began writing a letter to her grandmother.

Exercise WT 8

1. Harry and **I** are going shopping.

2. Are you going to give the ball to Tom or to **me**?

3. He gave Nanette and **me** the apples.

4. There are no secrets between you and **me**.

5. He didn't hide from Peter; he hid from **me**.

Clichés

Exercise WT 9

1. Learn as much as you can during your life, that's what my mother always told me.

2. You'll never get anywhere in life if you don't finish what you start.

3. People often say you'll be rewarded or disappointed, depending on how you behave.

4. He says that his children are always expecting him to help him, even though he does the best by them that he can.

5. That girl annoys me very much to the extent that she's always on my mind.

6. She might act as though she's young, but in fact is an aged pensioner.

Alliteration

 Exercise WT 10

1. Trains travel on tried and true tracks.
2. Ducks dive and dance by the docks.
3. Tom took ten troublesome turtles to town.
4. Poor Peter pounded his pinky painfully.
5. Many men marched up the mountain.
6. Lucky Luke looked longingly at long-legged Lucy.
7. Gavin gave Grace good grapes for growing in the garden.
8. More monkeys made matters more menacing.

Similes and Metaphors

 Exercise WT 11

1. Simile
2. Simile
3. Metaphor
4. Simile
5. Metaphor
6. Simile
7. Simile
8. Metaphor
9. Metaphor
10. Metaphor

Personification

 Exercise WT 12

1. The Sun smiled upon the children as the played by the river.
2. The plants were begging to be watered.
3. The angry clouds darkened the sky.
4. The stars danced in the moonlit night.
5. The wind played with my hair.

Ambiguity

Exercise WT 13

1. Catching the bus this morning, I noticed a kangaroo.

2. She bought a sofa with wobbly legs from the man.

3. He wore a hat made of felt on his head.

4. After breakfast, Dad announced that he was building a factory.

5. In the concert, we sang a tune about a man who fell in love.

6. The lady hit the man who was holding an umbrella.

7. Toni gave food to her cat.

8. The school is looking for teachers of French, German and Japanese.

9. Did you see the girl who was using the telescope?

10. The chicken is ready to eat some worms.

11. I looked at the one-eyed dog.

12. The teacher said he would test his students on Monday.

Overworked Words

Exercise WT 14

1. We ate a well-cooked pot roast.

2. Look at what I received from my best friend!

3. It's a priceless necklace.

4. You look so attractive in that dress.

5. We travelled to Canada by plane and then by train.

6. I had a horrifying time last night at the haunted house.

7. My brother's behaviour is delinquent.

8. I always have a fun-filled time at Adventure World.

9. My aunt caught the flu from her cat.

10. He was successful in his exams.

11. The fireworks were breathtaking.

12. She is such a considerate girl to take her little brother to the movies.

VOCABULARY

Synonyms

 Exercise VT 1

1. leave, desert
2. gain, benefit
3. rough, vulgar
4. cure, antidote
5. outside, outer
6. odd, charming
7. twilight, sundown
8. weariness, lethargy
9. thin, skinny
10. copy, emulate

Antonyms

Exercise VT 2

1. divide, decrease
2. loss, defeat
3. poor, destitute
4. expensive, costly
5. foe, enemy
6. contract, shrink
7. guilty, culpable
8. hell, agony
9. awake, attentive
10. wild, violent

Homonyms and homophones

Exercise VT 3

1. The **boy** tied his dinghy to the harbour **buoy**.
2. A large **herd** of animals was **heard** moving through the jungle.
3. The **plane** had to make a forced landing on the coastal **plain**.
4. Have you heard the **tale** about the dog's **tail**?
5. There was a **great** fire burning in the **grate**.
6. They **would** do all they could to save the **wood** being cut.
7. That woman **rode** all day along the dusty **road**.
8. I don't know **whether** to go out in the bad **weather** today.
9. **Their** books are on the desk over **there**.
10. I don't know if I can **bear** to see my sister **bare** in the shower.

Prefixes

 Exercise VT 4

1. **un**healthy
2. **un**truthful
3. **in**attentive
4. **in**experienced
5. **dis**respectful
6. **un**satisfied
7. **im**polite
8. **in**visible
9. **dis**loyal
10. **un**certain

Exercise VT 5

1. **re**play
2. **mis**lead
3. **anti**septic
4. **con**join
5. **tri**angle
6. **extra**ordinary
7. **sub**marine
8. **hemi**sphere
9. **dia**gram
10. **inter**national

Suffixes

 Exercise VT 6

1. disappoint**ment**
2. beaut**iful**
3. ugli**ness**
4. peace**able**
5. water**y**
6. notice**able**
7. point**ing**
8. hero**ic**
9. print**ed**
10. patriot**ism**
11. applica**tion**
12. nomin**ee**
13. help**ful**
14. weak**ness**
15. abilit**y**
16. child**ish**
17. tast**y**
18. conclus**ion**
19. clarifica**tion**
20. rela**tive**

Baby animals

 Exercise VT 7

1. squab
2. maggot
3. eaglet
4. cygnet
5. child, baby
6. foal
7. kid
8. kitten
9. peachick
10. duckling

Who lives there?

 Exercise VT 8

1. den
2. burrow or warren
3. hostel
4. convent or nunnery
5. barracks
6. monastery
7. den
8. igloo
9. lodge
10. coop

People's occupations

 Exercise VT 9

1. manager
2. translator
3. botanist
4. dramatist or playwright
5. engineer
6. exporter
7. game-keeper
8. warder
9. astrologer
10. author

Receptacles

 Exercise VT 10

1. caddy
2. shrine
3. scabbard or sheath
4. quiver
5. urn
6. satchel or brief case
7. locker
8. holster
9. flask
10. creel

Places

 Exercise VT 11

1. crematorium
2. shipyard
3. museum
4. stadium
5. distillery
6. granary
7. surgery
8. orphanage
9. vineyard
10. nursery

Forming nouns

 Exercise VT 12

1. perfection
2. heaven
3. emptiness
4. equality
5. death
6. circle
7. chief; chieftain
8. use
9. valuables
10. younger

Forming verbs

 Exercise VT 13

1. authorise
2. except
3. acquit
4. laugh
5. convenience
6. expect
7. victimise
8. wait
9. reflect
10. search

Forming adjectives

 Exercise VT 14

1. doting
2. culminating
3. indicating
4. loving; lovely
5. rejoicing
6. speaking
7. connecting
8. suitable
9. waiting
10. angry

Index

About the Author

Dianne (Di) Bates worked on the editorial team of the NSW Department of Education *School Magazine* after years as a classroom teacher. She co-edited the national children's magazines *Puffinalia and Little Ears*, worked as a writer-in-residence and tutor at numerous institutions, toured with the National Book Council of Australia, worked as a print media journalist and edited a weekly provincial newspaper and several online magazines.

Di is the author of over 120 books, including *The New Writer's Survival Guide* (Penguin), *Revise, Edit and Rewrite: A Guide to Improving Students' Writing* (Scholastic Australia), *How to Self-Edit to Improve Writing* (Five Senses Education) and *Wordgames: Activities for Creative Thinking and Writer* (Five Senses Education).

Di received Writer's Fellowships from the Literature Board of the Australia Council, has won national and state writing awards and has had her books translated overseas. She lives near Wollongong on the east coast of Australia with her author husband, Bill Condon.

Milton Keynes UK
Ingram Content Group UK Ltd.
UKHW050857040324
438885UK00012B/695